PRISM

READING AND WRITING
TEACHER'S MANUAL

Intro

Sabina Ostrowska

Kate Adams

with
Wendy Asplin
Christina Cavage
Jeanne Lambert

CAMBRIDGE
UNIVERSITY PRESS

CAMBRIDGE
UNIVERSITY PRESS

University Printing House, Cambridge CB2 8BS, United Kingdom

One Liberty Plaza, 20th Floor, New York, NY 10006, USA

477 Williamstown Road, Port Melbourne, VIC 3207, Australia

4843/24, 2nd Floor, Ansari Road, Daryaganj, Delhi – 110002, India

79 Anson Road, #06–04/06, Singapore 079906

Cambridge University Press is part of the University of Cambridge.

It furthers the University's mission by disseminating knowledge in the pursuit of education, learning and research at the highest international levels of excellence.

www.cambridge.org
Information on this title: www.cambridge.org/9781316624975

© Cambridge University Press 2017

First published 2017

20 19 18 17 16 15 14 13 12 11 10 9 8 7 6 5 4 3 2 1

Printed in Malaysia by Vivar Printing

A catalogue record for this publication is available from the British Library

ISBN 978-1-316-62497-5 Teacher's Manual Intro Reading and Writing
ISBN 978-1-316-62418-0 Student's Book with Online Workbook Intro Reading and Writing

CONTENTS

SCOPE AND SEQUENCE

UNIT	WATCH AND LISTEN	READINGS	READING SKILLS	LANGUAGE DEVELOPMENT	
1 PEOPLE *Academic Disciplines* Communications / Sociology	Thai Fishermen	1: Profile of Jeremy Lin (personal profile) 2: A Very Tall Man! (book excerpt)	*Key Skill* Previewing *Additional Skills* Understanding key vocabulary Skimming Scanning to find information Reading for details Synthesizing	Family vocabulary Nouns and verbs • Singular and plural nouns	
2 CLIMATE *Academic Disciplines* Geography / Meteorology	The Growing Ice Cap	1: The Coldest City in the World (article) 2: Cuba Weather (website)	*Key Skill* Scanning to find information *Additional Skills* Using your knowledge Understanding key vocabulary Reading for details Previewing Synthesizing	Nouns and adjectives Noun phrases	
3 LIFESTYLE *Academic Disciplines* Anthropology / Education	Panama's Kuna People	1: Meet the Kombai (book review) 2: Student schedule (class schedule)	*Key Skill* Annotating a text *Additional Skills* Using your knowledge Understanding key vocabulary Previewing Scanning to find information Reading for main ideas Synthesizing	Collocations for free-time activities Vocabulary for study Time expressions	
4 PLACES *Academic Disciplines* Geography / History	The Cenotes of Mexico	1: A World History of Maps (excerpts from a history book) 2: The Maldives: An Overview (fact file)	*Key Skill* Reading for main ideas *Additional Skills* Understanding key vocabulary Previewing Using your knowledge Annotating Scanning to find information Reading for details Synthesizing	Superlative adjectives Noun phrases with *of* Vocabulary for places	

CRITICAL THINKING	GRAMMAR FOR WRITING	WRITING	ON CAMPUS
Analyzing and using a two-column chart	Subject pronouns The verb *be* Possessive adjectives	*Academic Writing Skill* Writing simple sentences *Rhetorical Mode* Descriptive *Writing Task* Write a profile of someone in your family. (sentences)	*Life Skill* Meeting people
Understanding and using a three-column chart	Prepositional phrases	*Academic Writing Skills* Capital letters Commas *Rhetorical Mode* Descriptive *Writing Task* Write about the weather in your city or town. (sentences)	*Life Skill* Using English measurements
Analyzing and organizing information	Parts of a sentence The simple present	*Academic Writing Skill* Main ideas and details *Rhetorical Mode* Descriptive *Writing Task* Write about the life of a student in your class. (sentences)	*Study Skill* Creating a test study plan
Classifying key words	*There is / There are* Articles	*Academic Writing Skill* Paragraph structure • Topic sentences *Rhetorical Mode* Descriptive *Writing Task* Write facts about your country. (paragraph)	*Life Skill* Places on campus

UNIT	WATCH AND LISTEN	READINGS	READING SKILLS	LANGUAGE DEVELOPMENT	
5 JOBS *Academic Disciplines* Business / Career Services	Utah's Bingham Mine	1: Find_my_job.com (web page) 2: Email chain about jobs (emails)	*Key Skill* Reading for details *Additional Skills* Using your knowledge Understanding key vocabulary Scanning to find information Reading for main ideas Synthesizing	Vocabulary for jobs Adjective phrases	
6 HOMES AND BUILDINGS *Academic Disciplines* Architecture / Engineering	To Build the Tallest	1: Architect's World: Expert Interview (article) 2: Skyscrapers (article)	*Key Skill* Predicting content using visuals *Additional Skills* Using your knowledge Understanding key vocabulary Scanning to find information Reading for main ideas Reading for details Synthesizing	Pronouns Vocabulary for buildings Adjectives	
7 FOOD AND CULTURE *Academic Disciplines* History / Sociology	Goat Cheese	1: Tea: A World History (article) 2: 10 of the Best by Cuisine (travel guide)	*Key Skill* Taking notes *Additional Skills* Using your knowledge Understanding key vocabulary Reading for main ideas Reading for details Scanning to find information Synthesizing	Vocabulary about food Count and noncount nouns	
8 TRANSPORTATION *Academic Disciplines* Engineering / Urban Planning	Modern Subways	1: Transportation survey (survey) 2: Transportation in Bangkok: Report (student report)	*Key Skill* Skimming *Additional Skills* Previewing Understanding key vocabulary Skimming Scanning to find information Reading for details Using your knowledge Reading for main ideas Synthesizing	Quantifiers Transportation collocations	

CRITICAL THINKING	GRAMMAR FOR WRITING	WRITING	ON CAMPUS
Using a Likert scale to evaluate and analyze	The pronoun *you* *Must* and *have to*	**_Academic Writing Skills_** Joining ideas with *and* • Simple sentences • Writing compound sentences with *and* Writing an email **_Rhetorical Mode_** Descriptive **_Writing Task_** Write an email about a job. (paragraph)	**_Communication Skill_** Writing emails to professors
Comparing and using data	Comparing quantities Comparative adjectives	**_Academic Writing Skills_** Compound sentences with *but* Supporting sentences **_Rhetorical Mode_** Comparative **_Writing Task_** Write a comparison of two buildings. (paragraph)	**_Study Skill_** College classes
Brainstorming Using idea maps	Subject-verb agreement Determiners: *a*, *an*, and *some*	**_Academic Writing Skill_** Concluding sentences **_Rhetorical Mode_** Descriptive **_Writing Task_** Write about a popular food in your country. (paragraph)	**_Study Skill_** Making notes in a text
Collecting data using questionnaires and surveys Analyzing data	Sentence word order: subject-verb-object Linking sentences with pronouns	**_Academic Writing Skill_** Giving reasons with *because* and results with *so* **_Rhetorical Mode_** Explanatory **_Writing Task_** Write a paragraph explaining the results of a survey about transportation. (paragraph)	**_Life Skill_** Getting to campus and around town

INTRODUCTION

Prism **is a five-level paired skills series for beginner- to advanced-level students of North American English.** Its five Reading and Writing and five Listening and Speaking levels are designed to equip students with the language and skills to be successful both inside and outside of the college classroom.

Prism **uses a fresh approach to Critical Thinking based on a full integration of Bloom's taxonomy to help students become well-rounded critical thinkers.** The productive half of each unit begins with Critical Thinking. This section gives students the skills and tools they need to plan and prepare for success in their Speaking or Writing Task. Learners develop lower- and higher-order thinking skills, ranging from demonstrating knowledge and understanding to in-depth evaluation and analysis of content. Margin labels in the Critical Thinking sections highlight exercises that develop Bloom's concepts.

Prism **focuses on the most relevant and important language for students of academic English based on comprehensive research.** Key vocabulary is taken from the General Service List, the Academic Word List, and the Cambridge English Corpus. The grammar selected is also corpus-informed.

Prism **goes beyond language and critical thinking skills to teach students how to be successful, engaged college students both inside and outside of the classroom.** On Campus spreads at the end of each unit introduce students to communication, study, presentation, and life skills that will help them transition to life in North American community college and university programs.

Prism **combines print and digital solutions for the modern student and program.** Online workbooks give students additional graded language and skills practice. Video resources are available to students and teachers in the same platform. Presentation Plus gives teachers modern tools to enhance their students' learning environment in the classroom.

Prism **provides assessment resources for the busy teacher.** Photocopiable unit quizzes and answer keys are included in the Teacher's Manual, with downloadable PDF and Word versions available at Cambridge.org/prism and in the Resource tab of the Cambridge Learning Management System. Writing rubrics for grading Writing Tasks in the Student's Book and on the Unit Writing Quizzes are included in the Teacher's Manual.

SERIES LEVELS

Level	Description	CEFR Levels
Prism Intro	Beginner	A1
Prism 1	Low Intermediate	A2
Prism 2	Intermediate	B1
Prism 3	High Intermediate	B2
Prism 4	Advanced	C1

UNIT OPENER

Each unit opens with a striking two-page photo related to the topic, a Learning Objectives box, and an Activate Your Knowledge activity.

PURPOSE

- To introduce and generate interest in the unit topic with an engaging visual
- To set the learning objectives for the unit
- To make connections between students' background knowledge and the unit topic/theme

TEACHING SUGGESTIONS
PHOTO SPREAD

Lead an open class discussion on the connection between the unit opener photo and topic. Start off with questions like:
- *What is the first thing you notice in the photographs?*
- *What do you think of when you look at the photo?*
- *How is the photo connected to the unit title?*

ACTIVATE YOUR KNOWLEDGE

After students work in pairs to discuss the questions, have volunteers share with the class answers to questions that generated the most discussion.
You can also use the exercise to practice fluency. Instruct students to answer the questions as quickly as possible without worrying about creating grammatically correct sentences. Keep time and do not allow students more than 15–60 seconds per answer, depending on level and complexity of the question. You can then focus on accuracy when volunteers share their answers with the class.

WATCH AND LISTEN

Each unit includes a short authentic video from a respected news source that is related to the unit topic, along with exercises for students to do before, during, and after watching. The video can be played in the classroom or watched outside of class by students via the Cambridge LMS.
Note: A glossary defines above-level or specialized words that appear in the video and are essential for students to understand the main ideas so that teachers do not have to spend time pre-teaching or explaining this vocabulary while viewing.

PURPOSE

- To create a varied and dynamic learning experience
- To generate further interest in and discussion of the unit topic
- To build background knowledge and ideas on the topic
- To develop and practice key skills in prediction, comprehension, and discussion
- To personalize and give opinions on a topic

TEACHING SUGGESTIONS
PREPARING TO WATCH

Have students work in pairs to answer the Activating Your Knowledge exercise. Then have volunteers share their answers. For a livelier class discussion, answer the questions together as a class.
Students can complete the Predicting Content Using Visuals exercise on their own and then compare answers with a partner.

WHILE WATCHING

Watch the video twice, once while students listen for main ideas and once while they listen for key details. After each viewing, facilitate a discussion of students' answers and clarify any confusion. If some students still have trouble with comprehension, suggest that they watch the video again at home or during a computer lab session.

DISCUSSION

Have students work in pairs or small groups to answer the discussion questions. Have students compare their answers with another pair or group. Then have volunteers share their answers with the class. If possible, expand on their answers by making connections between their answers and the video content. For example: *That's an interesting perspective. How is it similar to what the speaker in the video mentioned? How is it different?*
For writing practice, have students write responses to the questions for homework.

READING

The first half of each unit focuses on the receptive skill of reading. Each unit includes two reading passages that provide different angles, viewpoints, and/or genres related to the unit topic.

READING 1

Reading 1 includes a reading passage on an academically related topic. It provides information on the unit topic, and it gives students exposure to and practice with language and reading skills while helping them begin to generate ideas for their Writing Task.

PREPARING TO READ

PURPOSE

- To prepare students to understand the content of the reading
- To introduce, review, and/or practice key pre-reading skills
- To introduce and build key academically related and topical vocabulary for the reading and for the unit Writing Task

TEACHING SUGGESTIONS

Encourage students to complete the pre-reading activities in this section in pairs or groups. This will promote a high level of engagement. Once students have completed the activities, check for understanding and offer any clarification.
Encourage or assign your students to keep a vocabulary notebook for new words. This should include new key vocabulary words, parts of speech, definitions (in the students' own words), and contextual sentences. To extend the vocabulary activity in this section, ask students to find synonyms, antonyms, or related terms for the vocabulary items they just practiced. These can then be added to their vocabulary notebooks.
Key vocabulary exercises can also be assigned ahead of time so that you can focus on the reading content and skills in class.
If time permits, have students scan Reading 1 for the key vocabulary just practiced in bold and read the sentences with each term. This will provide additional pre-reading scaffolding.

WHILE READING

PURPOSE

- To introduce, review, and/or practice key academic reading skills
- To practice reading comprehension and annotation skills
- To see and understand key vocabulary in a natural academically related context
- To provide information and stimulate ideas on an academically related topic
- To help students become more efficient readers

TEACHING SUGGESTIONS

Have students work in pairs or small groups to complete the activities. Students should always be prepared to support their answers from the text, so encourage them to annotate the text as they complete the activities. After students complete the activities, have volunteers share their answers with the class, along with support from the text. If necessary, facilitate clarification by referring back to the text yourself. Use guided questions to help with understanding. For example: *Take a moment to review the final sentences of Paragraph 2. What words discuss a problem?*

DISCUSSION

PURPOSE

- To give students the opportunity to discuss and offer opinions about what they read
- To think critically about the content of the reading
- To further personalize the topic and issues in Reading 1

TEACHING SUGGESTIONS

Give students three to five minutes to discuss and jot down notes for their answers before discussing them in pairs or small groups. Monitor student groups, taking notes on common mistakes. Then, survey the students on their favorite questions and have groups volunteer to share these answers. You can provide oral or written feedback on common mistakes at the end of the section.

READING 2

Reading 2 is a reading passage on the unit topic from a different angle and often in a different format than Reading 1. It gives students additional exposure to and practice with language and reading skills while helping them generate and refine ideas for their Writing Task. It generally includes rhetorical elements that serve as a structured model for the Writing Task.

PREPARING TO READ

PURPOSE

- To prepare students to understand the content of the reading
- To introduce, review, and/or practice key pre-reading skills
- To introduce and build key academically related and topical vocabulary for the reading and for the unit Writing Task

TEACHING SUGGESTIONS

As with Reading 1, encourage students to complete the activities in this section in pairs or small groups to promote a high level of engagement. Circulate among students at this time, taking notes of common areas of difficulty. Once students have completed the activities, check for understanding and offer clarification, paying particular attention to any problem areas you noted.

If you wish to extend the vocabulary activity in this section, elicit other word forms of the key vocabulary. Students can add these word forms to their vocabulary notebooks.

WHILE READING

PURPOSE

- To introduce, review, and/or practice key academic reading skills
- To practice reading comprehension and annotation skills
- To see and understand key vocabulary in a natural academically related context
- To provide information and stimulate ideas on an academically related topic
- To help students become more efficient readers
- To model aspects or elements of the Writing Task

TEACHING SUGGESTIONS

As with Reading 1, have students work in pairs or small groups to complete the activities. Encourage them to annotate the reading so that they are prepared to support their answers from the text. Elicit answers and explanations from the class. Remember to facilitate clarification by referring back to the text yourself, using clear, guided questions to help with understanding.

Alternatively, separate the class into multiple groups, and assign a paragraph or section of the reading to each groups. (Students should skim the rest of the passage not assigned to them.) Set a time limit for reading. Then do the exercises as a class, with each group responsible for answering and explaining the items that fall within their paragraph or section of the text.

DISCUSSION

PURPOSE

- To personalize and expand on the ideas and content of Reading 2
- To practice synthesizing the content of the unit reading passages

TEACHING SUGGESTIONS

Before students discuss the questions in this section the first time, introduce the key skill of synthesis. Start by defining synthesis (combining and analyzing ideas from multiple sources). Stress its importance in higher education: in college or graduate school, students will be asked to synthesize ideas from a wide range of sources, to think critically about them, to make connections among them, and to add their own ideas. Note: you may need to review this information periodically with your class.

Have students answer the questions in pairs or small groups, and then ask for volunteers to share their answers with the class. Facilitate the discussion, encouraging students to make connections between Reading 1 and Reading 2. If applicable, ask students to relate the content of the unit video to this section. This is also a good context in which to introduce the Writing Task at the beginning of the Critical Thinking section and to have students consider how the content of the reading passages relates to the prompt.

To extend this activity beyond discussion, write the connections students make on the board, and have students take notes. Students can then use their notes to write sentences or a paragraph(s) describing how the ideas in all the sources discussed are connected.

LANGUAGE DEVELOPMENT

Each unit includes the introduction and practice of academically related language relevant to the unit topic and readings, and useful for the unit Writing Task. The focus of this section is on vocabulary and/or grammar.

PURPOSE

- To recycle and expand on vocabulary that appears in Reading 1 or Reading 2
- To focus and expand on grammar that appears in Reading 1 or Reading 2
- To expose students to additional corpus-informed, research-based language for the unit topic and level
- To practice language and structures that students can use in the Writing Task

TEACHING SUGGESTIONS

For grammar points, review the language box as a class and facilitate answers to any unclear sections. Alternatively, have students review it in pairs and allow time for questions. Then have students work in pairs to complete the accompanying activities. Review students' answers, allowing time for any clarification.

For vocabulary points, have students complete the exercises in pairs. Then, review answers and allow time for any clarification. To extend this activity, have students create sentences using each term and/or make a list of synonyms, antonyms, or related words and phrases for each term. Students should also add relevant language to their vocabulary notebooks. For homework, have students annotate the readings in the unit, underlining or highlighting any language covered in this section.

WRITING

The second half of each unit focuses on the productive skill of writing. It begins with the prompt for the Writing Task and systematically equips students with the grammar and skills to plan for, prepare, and execute the task successfully.

CRITICAL THINKING

PURPOSE

- To introduce the Writing Task.
- To notice and analyze features of Reading 2 related to the Writing Task
- To help generate, develop, and organize ideas for the Writing Task.
- To teach and practice the lower-order critical thinking skills of remembering, understanding, and applying knowledge through practical brainstorming and organizational activities
- To teach and practice the higher-order critical thinking skills of analyzing, evaluating, and creating in order to prepare students for success in the Writing Task and, more generally, in the college classroom

TEACHING SUGGESTIONS

Encourage students to work through this section collaboratively in pairs or small groups to promote a high level of engagement. Facilitate their learning and progress by circulating and checking in on students as they work through this section. If time permits, have groups exchange and evaluate one another's work.
Note: Students will often be directed back to this section to review, revise, and expand on their initial ideas and notes for the Writing Task.

GRAMMAR FOR WRITING

PURPOSE

- To introduce and practice grammar that is relevant to the Writing Task
- To introduce and practice grammar that often presents trouble for students at this level of academically related writing

TEACHING SUGGESTIONS

Review any skills boxes in this section as a class, allowing time to answer questions and clarify points of confusion. Then have students work on the activities in pairs or small groups, before eliciting answers as a class.

ACADEMIC WRITING SKILLS

PURPOSE

- To present and practice academic writing skills needed to be successful in college or graduate school
- To focus on specific language and skills relevant to the Writing Task

Have students read any skills boxes on their own. Check understanding by asking guided questions like:

- *What do you notice about the parallel structure examples?*
- *What are some other examples of parallel structure?*
- *How would you describe parallel structure based on the information and examples you just read?*

Provide clarification as necessary, offering and eliciting more examples. Have students find examples in the unit readings if possible.

Students can work in pairs to complete the exercises and then share their answers with the class. Alternatively, assign exercises for homework.

WRITING TASK

PURPOSE

- To work collaboratively in preparation for the Writing Task
- To revisit, revise, and expand on work done in the Critical Thinking section
- To provide an opportunity for students to synthesize the language, skills, and ideas presented and generated in the unit
- To help students plan, draft, and edit their writing

TEACHING SUGGESTIONS

Depending on time and class level, students can complete the preparation activities for homework or in class. If conducted in class, have students work on their own to complete the Plan section. They can then share their plans in pairs. Give students time to revise their plans based on feedback from their partners.

Depending on time, students can write their first drafts at home or in class. Encourage students to refer to the Task Checklist after writing their first drafts. The checklist can also be used in a peer review of first drafts in class. Students should then edit their writing based on feedback from the peer review.

Even with a peer review, it is important to provide written feedback for your students. When doing so, look for common mistakes in student writing. Select at least one problem sentence or area from each student's draft, and conduct an edit correction exercise either as a class or in an online discussion forum. You can also select and review a well-written sentence from each draft to serve as models and to provide positive reinforcement.

Note: For the first unit or two, you may want to conduct the writing task as a collaborative class activity. You can elicit sentences from students and write them on the board, or have students come to the board and write sentences themselves. Use guiding questions and the Task Checklist to help students edit the sentences.

ON CAMPUS

Each unit concludes with a unique spread that teaches students concepts and skills that go beyond traditional reading and writing academic skills.

PURPOSE

- To familiarize students with all aspects of the North American college experience
- To enable students to interact and participate successfully in the college classroom
- To prepare students to navigate typical North American college campus life

TEACHING SUGGESTIONS

PREPARING TO READ

Have students read the skills box silently. Then begin with an open discussion by asking students what they know about the topic. For example:

- *What is a study plan?*
- *Have you ever written an email to a teacher or professor?*
- *How do college students choose a major?*
- *What is a virtual classroom?*

You can also write the question on the board and assign as pair work, and have students share their answers with the class.

WHILE READING

Have students read the text and complete the accompanying activities. Elicit from some volunteers how the reading relates to what they read in the skills box. Have them read again and check their work. You can extend these activities by asking the following questions:

- *What did you find most interesting in this reading passage?*
- *What did you understand more clearly during the second reading?*
- *Who do you think wrote the text? Why?*

PRACTICE

Give students two minutes to discuss the information from the reading with partners before they complete the exercises. Elicit from some volunteers how the exercises practice what they read in the text.

REAL-WORLD APPLICATION

Depending on time, you may want to assign the activities in this section as homework. Having students collaborate on these real-world tasks either inside or outside of the classroom simulates a common practice in college and graduate school. At the beginning of the week you can set up a schedule so that several student groups present their work during class throughout the week.

To extend this section, assign small related research projects, as applicable. For example, have students research and report on three websites with information on choosing a college major.

PRISM WRITING TASK RUBRIC

CATEGORY	CRITERIA	SCORE
Content and Development	• Writing completes the task and fully answers the prompt. • Content is meaningful and interesting. • Main points and ideas are fully developed with good support and logic.	

Organization	• Writing is well-organized and follows the conventions of academic writing:
	  • Sentences – word order, no fragments or run-ons
	  • Paragraph – topic sentence, supporting details, concluding sentence
	• Rhetorical mode used is appropriate to the writing task.	

Coherence, Clarity, and Unity	• Sentences within a paragraph flow logically with appropriate transitions. • Sentences and ideas are clear and make sense to the reader. • All sentences in a paragraph relate to the topic sentence.	
Vocabulary	• Vocabulary, including expressions and transition language, is accurate, appropriate, and varied. • Writing shows mastery of unit key vocabulary and Language Development.	
Grammar and Writing Skills	• Grammar is accurate, appropriate, and varied. • Writing shows mastery of unit Grammar for Writing and Language Development. • Sentence types are varied and used appropriately. • Level of formality shows an understanding of audience and purpose. • Mechanics (capitalization, punctuation, indentation, and spelling) are strong. • Writing shows mastery of unit Academic Writing Skills.	

How well does the response meet the criteria?	Recommended Score
At least 90%	20
At least 75%	15
At least 60%	10
At least 50%	5
Less than 50%	0
Total Score Possible per Section	20
Total Score Possible	100

Feedback:

UNIT 1
ACIVATE YOUR KNOWLEDGE

Exercise 1 page 15
Answers will vary.

WATCH AND LISTEN

Exercise 1 page 16
Answers will vary.

Exercise 2 page 16
1 There are houses near the water.
2 The boys are getting on a boat.
3 The boys are jumping in the water.
4 He is swimming in the sea.

Exercise 3 page 17
1 2 4 6

Exercise 4 page 17
1 village   2 equipment   3 jump   4 friends
5 family

Exercise 5 page 17
1 children   2 fish   3 boat
4 they learn how to see underwater.

Exercise 6 page 17
Answers will vary.

READING 1

Exercise 1 page 18
1 Information about a person and their life
2 Facebook and other social and work web sites
3 A basketball player

Exercise 2 page 18
1 city
2 languages
3 country
4 date of birth
5 job
6 hobbies

Exercise 3 page 20
1 Contact information
2 My family
3 My hobbies
4 My life

Exercise 4 page 20
1 the United States
2 basketball
3 playing the piano and video games
4 interest

5 mother
6 father
7 jeremy.lin@cup.org
8 Harvard University

Exercise 5 page 20
1 basketball player
2 Torrance, California
3 1988
4 speaks
5 brothers

Exercise 6 page 20
Answers will vary.

READING 2

Exercise 1 page 21
1 a
2 c
3 a

Exercise 2 page 21
1 f
2 c
3 g
4 d
5 e
6 h
7 b
8 a

Exercise 3 page 23
1 Sultan
2 Kösen
3 Turkey
4 Mardin
5 1 sister and 3 brothers
6 watching TV

Exercise 4 page 23
1 is
2 lives
3 family
4 is
5 watching
6 speaks

Exercise 5 page 23
1 People look at him. Normal clothes and shoes are too small.
2 Jeremy is interested in helping young people. Sultan is interested in music.
3 You learn the name, job, and hobbies of a person. You learn about their family and where the person lives.
4 *Answers will vary.*

LANGUAGE DEVELOPMENT

Exercise 1 page 24
1 brother
2 grandfather
3 uncle
4 mother
5 daughter

Exercise 2 page 24
Nouns: Taiwan, basketball, languages
Verbs: lives, works, is, plays

Exercise 3 page 25
1 sisters
2 aunt
3 grandfather
4 sons
5 brothers

Exercise 4 page 25
1 plays
2 sister
3 languages
4 brothers
5 lives
6 city

CRITICAL THINKING

Exercise 1 page 26
1 Kösen
2 Mardin
3 his mother, his three brothers, and his sister
4 farmer
5 watching TV/interested in music
6 Turkish and English

Exercise 2 page 26
Answers will vary.

Exercise 3 page 26
Answers will vary.

GRAMMAR FOR WRITING

Exercise 1 page 27
she: daughter, mother
he: brother, father, grandfather
they: sons, aunts, uncles, sisters

Exercise 2 page 27
1 She
2 They

Exercise 3 page 29
A
1 is
2 am
3 am
4 is
5 is
6 is
7 is
8 is
B
1 am
2 am
3 is
4 are
5 is
6 is
7 is
8 are

Exercise 4 page 29
1 am not
2 are not / aren't
3 is not / isn't
4 is not / isn't
5 are not / aren't
6 are not / aren't

Exercise 5 page 30
1 Their
2 Her
3 Our
4 My
5 His
6 Its

ACADEMIC WRITING SKILLS

Exercise 1 page 31
1 My grandfather's name is Zhong Shan.
2 He is 59
3 He is a doctor.
4 He is from Hong Kong.
5 He has two daughters.
6 He lives with my mother and father.

Exercise 2 page 32
1 My name is Gustavo.
2 I am from Ecuador.
3 I am 19.
4 My father's name is Marcus.
5 He is a teacher.
6 He has two sons.
7 My brother's name is Paulo.
8 He is a doctor.
9 He is in Canada. / He lives in Canada.
10 Paulo's hobbies are playing the piano and watching TV.

WRITING TASK

Exercises 1–5 pages 32–33
Answers will vary.

ON CAMPUS

Exercise 1 page 34
Answers will vary.

Exercise 3 page 35
1 b
2 a
3 b
4 b

Exercise 4 page 35
1 the International Student Club
2 No
3 12

Exercises 5–8 page 35
Answers will vary.

UNIT 2
ACIVATE YOUR KNOWLEDGE

Exercise 1 page 37
Answers will vary.

WATCH AND LISTEN

Exercise 1 page 38
Answers will vary.

Exercise 2 page 38
1 F; This part of the Earth is cold.
2 T
3 T
4 F; the trees can live in cold temperatures.

Exercise 3 page 39
1 2 3 5

Exercise 4 page 39
1 south   2 cold   3 30%   4 snow

Exercise 5 page 39
1 winter   2 near   3 difficult   4 flowers

Exercise 6 page 39
Answers will vary.

READING 1

Exercise 1 page 40
1 b
2 a
3 c

Exercise 2 page 40
1 f
2 b
3 e
4 d
5 g
6 a
7 c

Exercise 3 page 40
Answers will vary.

Exercise 4 page 40
1 T
2 T
3 F; Summer is warm in Yakutsk.
4 F; Svetlana has a café in Yakutsk.

Exercise 5 page 42
1 f
2 b
3 a
4 c
5 e
6 d

Exercise 6 page 42
1 Svetlana
2 Yakutsk
3 cold
4 spring
5 warm

Exercise 7 page 42
Answers will vary.

READING 2

Exercise 1 page 43
Answers will vary.

Exercise 2 page 43
1 c
2 b
3 c

Exercise 3 page 43
1 rainfall
2 season
3 dry
4 climate

Exercise 4 page 44
1 cloudy
2 rainy
3 sunny
4 windy

Exercise 5 page 45
1 e
2 c
3 f
4 d
5 a
6 b

Exercise 6 page 45
Possible answers:
1 April or May; dry weather and warm temperatures
2 The dry season and the rainy season
3 The Internet, guide books, tourist information brochures
4 *Answers will vary but may include*: so they can plan activities, what to wear, etc.

LANGUAGE DEVELOPMENT

Exercise 1 page 45
1 Noun: café; Adjective: warm
2 Noun: October; Adjective: rainy
3 Noun: climate; Adjective: good
4 Noun: Summers; Adjective: hot
5 Noun: Winters; Adjective: cold

Exercise 2 page 46
1 difficult
2 happy
3 sunny
4 cold
5 cloudy

Exercise 3 page 46
1 cold winters
2 dry season
3 high rainfall
4 warm summers

Exercise 4 page 46
1 Cuba has a rainy season.
2 Yakutsk has a cold fall.
3 In the summer, we have sunny weather.
4 The dry season is windy.
5 In spring, the rainfall is high.

CRITICAL THINKING

Exercise 1 page 47

A	B	C
seasons	months	average temperatures (°F)
winter	December, January, February	–44
spring	March, April, May	–6
summer	June, July, August	68
fall	September, October, November	–6

Exercise 2 page 48
1 Yes
2 Yes
3 Cold
4 September, October, November
5 Cold but warmer than winter

Exercise 3 page 48
Answers will vary.

Exercise 4 page 48
Answers will vary.

GRAMMAR FOR WRITING

Exercise 1 page 49
1 in
2 in
3 between
4 in; about
5 for

Exercise 2 page 50
1 In the dry season
2 in the dry season

Exercise 3 page 50
1 sentence 1
2 between

Exercise 4 page 50
1 in July
2 In the rainy season,
3 in the dry season

Exercise 5 page 51
1 In October, it is windy.
2 The weather is good in the summer.
3 In Cuba, the climate is good.
4 In the fall, the average rainfall is 13 inches (34 mm).
5 The winters are cold in Yakutsk.
6 The average temperature in the summer is 68 °F (20 °C).
7 In the dry season, the average rainfall is 26 inches (62mm).

ACADEMIC WRITING SKILLS

Exercise 1 page 53
1 It is spring in March, April, and May.
2 It rains in spring, summer, and fall.
3 The coldest months are December, January, and February.
4 The warmest months are June, July, and August.

Exercise 2 page 53
1 In January, the weather is cold in Russia.
2 The average temperature is 70 °F (21 °C) in July.
3 In the rainy season, the average rainfall is 57 inches (146 mm) in Cuba.
4 The weather is sunny in the summer.

WRITING TASK

Exercises 1–6 pages 54–55
Answers will vary.

ON CAMPUS

Exercise 1 page 56
Answers will vary.

Exercise 3 page 57
1 b
2 b
3 a
4 a

Exercise 4 page 57
1 34°F
2 16 ounces
3 21 years; 5 feet 2 inches
4 1 gallon
5 85 miles

Exercise 5 page 57
Answers will vary.

Exercise 6 page 57
Answers will vary.

UNIT 3
ACIVATE YOUR KNOWLEDGE

Exercise 1 page 59
1 In a café
2 They are studying and eating.
3 *Answers will vary.*
4 *Answers will vary.*

WATCH AND LISTEN

Exercise 1 page 60
Answers will vary.

Exercise 2 page 60
a 3 b 4 c 2 d 1

Exercise 3 page 61
2 3 4 6

Exercise 4 page 61
1 T
2 F; Kuna fishermen swim more than 100 feet deep.
3 T
4 F; They have small gardens around their homes.
5 F; In their free time, they often play music and dance.

Exercise 5 page 61
1 long 2 fish 3 music and dancing 4 land

Exercise 6 page 61
Answers will vary.

READING 1

Exercise 1 page 62
Answers will vary.

Exercise 2 page 62
a hunter, a jungle, a tree house,

Exercise 3 page 62
1 b
2 f
3 d
4 g
5 a
6 h
7 c
8 e

Exercise 4 page 64
2 Rebecca Moore
3 Kombai women
4 Kombai men, Kombai women, Kombai children
5 Kombai men, Kombai women, Kombai children
6 Kombai men, Kombai women
7 Kombai men, Kombai women, Kombai children
8 Rebecca Moore

Exercises 5–6 page 64
1 b
2 a
3 d
4 c

Exercise 7 page 64
1 *Possible answer*: Maybe it is safer to live in the trees. Maybe it floods and they need to live in the trees.
2 They teach their children to cook, hunt, and swim.
3 *Answers will vary.*

READING 2

Exercise 1 page 65
Answers will vary.

Exercise 2 page 65
1 a
2 b
3 b
4 a
5 a
6 b
7 a
8 a

Exercise 3 page 66
noun: schedule
verb: relax
adjective: busy
part of the day: morning, afternoon, evening
part of the week: weekday, weekend

Exercise 4 page 66
1 T
2 F; the schedule and text are from a planner.
3 T

Exercise 5 page 68
Possible answers:
Paragraph 1 student, busy schedule, five classes
Paragraph 2 weekday mornings, three classes
Paragraph 3 afternoon classes, evening library
Paragraph 4 weekend, relaxes, friends

Exercise 6 page 68
1 schedule
2 student
3 classes
4 morning
5 relaxes

Exercise 7 page 68
1 weekend; goes to the pool
2 *Answers will vary.*
3 *Answers will vary.*

LANGUAGE DEVELOPMENT

Exercise 1 page 69
1 b
2 c
3 e
4 a
5 d

Exercise 2 page 70
1 meets
2 take
3 go

4 have
5 eats
6 relax
7 cooks
8 do

Exercise 3 page 70
arts and humanities: history, art and design
business: economics
math and science: calculus, physics, biology, chemistry
language and writing: English composition

Exercise 4 page 71
1 calculus
2 English
3 physics
4 chemistry
5 history
6 biology
7 economics

Exercise 5 page 71
1 on; at
2 In
3 On; at
4 in
5 On; at
6 on
7 in
8 at

CRITICAL THINKING

Exercise 1 page 72
1 Taha
2 University of Michigan
3 physics, calculus, English, engineering, history
4 6 am
5 Every weekday morning: physics, calculus, engineering;
  Monday and Wednesday afternoon: English, Thursday
  afternoon: history
6 Friday afternoon
7 In the evenings
8 On the weekends

Exercise 2 page 72
Answers will vary.

GRAMMAR FOR WRITING

Exercise 1 page 73
1 b
2 a
3 d
4 c

Exercise 2 page 75

travels, goes, studies, stays, has

Exercise 3 page 75

1 is
2 is
3 studies
4 gets up
5 eats
6 meets
7 has
8 studies
9 goes
10 is

ACADEMIC WRITING SKILLS

Exercise 1 page 76

Main idea: Matteo has three classes every weekday morning.
Details: He gets up at 6 am every day. Then he has physics from 8 am to 9 am, calculus from 9:15 am to 10:15 am, and engineering from 10:30 am to 11:30 am.
1 a
2 b

Exercise 2 page 76

Main idea: On the weekends, Matteo relaxes with friends.
Details: Sometimes, he goes to the pool to swim. He enjoys his busy life.
Answers will vary. Possible answer: He also like to go to the gym.

WRITING TASK

Exercises 1–6 pages 76–77
Answers will vary.

ON CAMPUS

Exercise 1 page 78
Answers will vary.

Exercise 3 page 79

1 b
2 a
3 d
4 c

Exercise 4 page 79
Answers will vary.

Exercise 5 and Exercise 6 page 79
Answers will vary.

UNIT 4
ACIVATE YOUR KNOWLEDGE

Exercise 1 page 81
1 Grand Canyon
2 *Answers will vary.*
3 *Answers will vary.*
4 *Answers will vary.*

WATCH AND LISTEN

Exercise 1 page 82
Answers will vary.

Exercise 2 page 82
1 There is a monkey in the forest
2 There is a space in the trees.
3 Plants are growing in the water.
4 A man is swimming in the water

Exercise 3 page 83
2 5 6

Exercise 4 page 83
1 trees   2 special   3 Water   4 animals   5 cold

Exercise 5 page 83
1 very   2 need   3 is   4 dangerous

Exercise 6 page 83
Answers will vary.

READING 1

Exercise 1 page 84
1 c   2 b   3 b

Exercise 2 page 84
1 b   2 b   3 a   4 b   5 a   6 a   7 a

Exercise 3 page 86
1 Muhammad al-Idrisi
2 Tabula Rogeriana
3 Norway, Spain, Italy, India, and China
4 Mediterranean Sea, the Indian Ocean, the Nile river

Exercise 4 page 86
continents: Asia, Europe, Africa
countries: Spain, Norway, Morocco, China

Exercise 5 page 86
1 F; He was Moroccan / from Morocco.
2 F; It is written in Arabic.
3 T
4 T
5 T

Exercise 6 page 86
1 He used information from explorers.
2 Where people at that time thought mountains, rivers, lakes, seas, and countries were
3 They may show more details. They may be more exact.

READING 2

Exercise 1 page 87
Answers will vary.

Exercise 2 page 87
1 c
2 e
3 d
4 b
5 f
6 a
7 h
8 g

Exercise 3 page 89

Paragraph number	Topic (*suggested*)	Main idea
1	The Maldives	The Maldives are islands in the Indian Ocean.
2	People	There are 370,000 people in the Maldives.
3	The capital of the Maldives	The capital of the Maldives is Malé.
4	The languages of the Maldives	People in Malé speak English and Dhivehi.
5	Tourism and fishing	Tourism and fishing are the most important businesses in the Maldives.
6	Life on Malé	Life on my island is very simple.
7	Food in the Maldives	The Maldives are famous for its fish.
8	Free time activities in the Maldives	People in the Maldives like to swim and dive.

Exercise 4 page 89
1 for their good climate, beautiful beaches, and warm seas
2 *Answers will vary.*
3 *Answers will vary.*

LANGUAGE DEVELOPMENT

Exercise 1 page 90
2 The Missouri River in the United States is **the longest**.
3 We live in **the biggest** city in Colombia.
4 The beaches in the Maldives are **the most beautiful**.
5 **The most popular** dish in the Maldives is fish soup.

Exercise 2 page 91
1 d   2 e   3 a   4 c   5 b

Exercise 3 page 91

CRITICAL THINKING

Exercise 1 page 91
Geography: islands, climate, Indian Ocean, near Sri Lanka
Language: English, Dhivehi
Industry: tourism, fishing, currency

Exercise 2 page 91
Capital: Malé, modern city, international airport, harbor
Population: 370,000, small islands

Exercise 3 page 93
Answers will vary.

Exercise 4 page 93
Answers will vary.

GRAMMAR FOR WRITING

Exercise 1 page 94
1 There are different kinds of business in my country.
2 There are 36 languages in Senegal.
3 There are three modern airports in my city.
4 There is a big museum of art in Seoul.
5 There is a beautiful beach in my city.

Exercise 2 page 94

correct: 1, 4, 6,

wrong: 2, 3, 5, 7, 8

Exercise 3 page 94

2 There **are** mountains in Colorado.

3 There **are** many parks in San Francisco.

5 There **are** many people in Buenos Aires.

7 **There** are many lakes in Michigan.

8 **There** is a big river in my city.

Exercise 4 page 95

1 ∅

2 ∅, ∅

3 the

4 The

5 the

6 ∅, ∅

Exercise 5 page 96

1 I come from ~~the~~ India.

2 Paris is ~~an~~ popular city with tourists.

3 There is **a** very tall building in Abu Dhabi.

4 I go to ~~an~~ university in Boston.

5 **The** United Kingdom is in ~~a~~ Europe.

6 I live by **a** big lake

7 **The** Ural mountains are in Russia.

ACADEMIC WRITING SKILLS

Exercise 1 page 97

1 The Maldives are islands in the Indian Ocean.

2 Tourism and fishing are the most important businesses in the Maldives.

Exercise 2 page 98

1 a

2 b

Exercise 3 page 98

Answers will vary.

WRITING TASK

Exercises 1–5 pages 98–99

Answers will vary.

ON CAMPUS

Exercise 1 page 100

Answers will vary.

Exercise 3 page 100

	library	bookstore	writing center
What?	tour	sale	workshop
When?	every Wednesday at 1pm	March 4–11	every day
Where?	Study Room A	Information Desk	401 Smith Hall

Exercise 4 page 101

1 a librarian

2 online

3 dictionaries

4 no (students only)

Exercises 5 page 101

1 tutoring center

2 writing center

3 international student services

4 transportation center

5 housing office

6 health center

Exercises 6–8 page 101

Answers will vary.

UNIT 5
ACIVATE YOUR KNOWLEDGE

Exercise 1 page 103

1 construction workers

2–4 *Answers will vary.*

WATCH AND LISTEN

Exercise 1 page 104

Answers will vary.

Exercise 2 page 104

1 c   2 d   3 a   4 b

Exercise 3 page 105

1 T

2 F; The mine produces enough copper wires for all the homes in the USA and Mexico.

3 T

4 F; The trucks work 24 hours a day.

Exercise 4 page 105

1 largest   2 one mile   3 small   4 stronger

Exercise 5 page 105

1 2 4 5

Exercise 6 page 105

Answers will vary.

READING 1

Exercise 1 page 106

1–3 *Answers will vary.*

Exercise 2 page 106

b

Exercise 3 page 106

1 a   2 a   3 b   4 b   5 a   6 a   7 a   8 b

Exercise 4 page 108

1 nurse   2 teacher   3 Canada   4 United State
5 FlyHigh (air transport company)   6 $130-$180 per hour
7 $48,000 per year   8 September-June

Exercise 5 page 108

1 T
2 F; The teacher has to teach grade 1–3.
3 T
4 T
5 T
6 T

Exercise 6 page 108

1 B, C
2 A, B; patients and customers are from different
   countries.
3 *Answers will vary.*

READING 2

Exercise 1 page 109

Answers will vary.

Exercise 2 page 109

Answers will vary.

Exercise 3 page 109

1 h
2 b
3 g
4 e
5 d
6 c
7 a
8 f

Exercise 4 page 111

1 dance teacher
2 12
3 software engineer
4 $65,150
5 South Korea
6 10 to 12

Exercise 5 page 111

c

Exercise 6 page 111

1 M
2 D
3 E
4 M
5 D

Exercise 7 page 111

1–4 *Answers will vary.*

LANGUAGE DEVELOPMENT

Exercise 1–2 pages 112–113

A Jobs	B activities	C locations
1 A farmer	grows food and raises animals	on a farm.
2 A manager	manages people	in an office. / in a company.
3 A doctor	gives people medicine	in a hospital.
4 A journalist	writes news stories	in an office.
5 A software engineer	creates software for computers	in a company. / in an office.
6 A basketball player	plays on a sports team	in a center.
7 A school teacher	teaches children	in a school.
8 A dance teacher	teaches people to dance	in a school. / in a center.
9 A nurse	takes care of sick people	in a hospital.
10 A language teacher	teaches languages	in a school.

Exercise 3 page 113

1 healthy and strong
2 very smart
3 friendly
4 strong

Exercise 4 page 113

1 with
2 with
3 with
4 at
5 at

CRITICAL THINKING

Exercise 1 page 114
Answers will vary.

Exercise 2 page 115
1 healthy and in shape
2 good at dancing
3 good with people
4 very smart
5 kind and helpful
6 good with children
7 very good at basketball
8 good at math
9 good at writing
10 good with computers
11 good with animals
12 good at languages

Exercise 3 page 115
Answers may vary.
farmer = healthy and in shape
manager = good with people
doctor = very smart
journalist = good at writing
software engineer = good with computers
basketball player = very good at basketball
school teacher = good with children
dance teacher = good at dancing
nurse = kind and helpful, good with people/children
language teacher = good at languages

Exercise 4 page 115
Answers will vary.

GRAMMAR FOR WRITING

Exercise 1 page 116
1 You must have three years of experience.
2 You are kind and good with people.
3 You have a university education.
4 You speak Chinese.

Exercise 2 page 117
1 A basketball player **must** be strong and healthy.
2 Pilots have **to** work at night.
3 A manager **has** to be helpful.
4 Teachers must **be** good with people.
5 A software engineer must **be** good at math.
6 Farmers have **to be** good with animals.
7 Journalists must **be** good at writing.
8 A language teacher must **be** good at speaking and writing.

Exercise 3 page 117
1 A farmer does not have to be good with people.
2 A software engineer does not have to be patient and kind.
3 Nurses do not have to be good with animals.
4 You do not have to be strong.
5 A French teacher does not have to be good at math.
6 You do not have to be good at calculus.

ACADEMIC WRITING SKILLS

Exercise 1 page 118
1 You must be smart and good with people.
2 You have to be healthy and strong.
3 Dance teachers have to be in shape, and you are in shape.
4 The job is to teach English, and you are an English and French teacher.

Exercise 2 page 119
Answers will vary.

WRITING TASK

Exercises 1–5 pages 120–121
Answers will vary.

ON CAMPUS

Exercise 1 page 122
1 *Answers will vary.*
2 You are sick and you want to know the homework assignment.
You don't like your project group.
You want to turn in your homework late.
You need help with a lesson.
3 *Answers will vary.*

Exercise 3 page 123
1 to talk to her professor
2 1:30; she has to work during the professor's office hours
3 to turn in her project next week
4 she has a lot of homework and she has a test tomorrow

Exercise 4 page 123

Which student ...	Magda	Lily
a is polite?	✓	
b writes the class name?	✓	
c uses slang?		✓
d writes her full name?	✓	
e writes her professor's name?	✓	
f gives a good reason?	✓	

Exercises 5–8 page 123
Answers will vary.

UNIT 6
ACIVATE YOUR KNOWLEDGE

Exercise 1 page 125
Answers will vary.

WATCH AND LISTEN

Exercise 1 page 126
Answers will vary. Possible answers: Canada – CN Tower, Chateau Frontenac; Italy – Leaning Tower of Pisa, Colosseum; Mexico – Pyramids (Chichen Itza, Teotihuacan); Dubai, UAE – Burj Khalifa, Burj Al Arab; China – Shanghai Tower, Summer Palace, Great Wall

Exercise 2 page 126
a 2   b 4   c 3   d 1

Exercise 3 page 127
a 2   b 3   c 1   d 5   e 4

Exercise 4 page 127
1 455   2 The Great Pyramid   3 steel   4 concrete

Exercise 5 page 127
1 3 4 5 6

Exercise 6 page 127
Answers will vary.

READING 1

Exercise 1 page 128
Answers will vary.

Exercise 2 page 128
1 D
2 C
3 F
4 H
5 B
6 E
7 A
8 G

Exercise 3 page 129
Answers will vary. Most common answers will be a and c.

Exercise 4 page 130

	windows are different sizes	has glass walls	has a small garden on the roof	rooms are narrow
Japanese steep roof house	✓			✓
Vietnamese "garden home"		✓	✓	

Exercise 5 page 130
1 c   2 b   3 a

Exercise 6 page 130
1 F; Professor Chan's favorite home designs are Japanese.
2 T
3 F; Professor Chan says it is important to build houses that are good for the earth.
4 T
5 T
6 F; In Amsterdam, one architect put mirrors on the walls.

Exercise 7 page 130
1 *Answers will vary.*
2 *Answers will vary.*
3 Answers will vary but may include to do something different/exciting/interesting.

READING 2

Exercise 1 page 131
Answers will vary.

Exercise 2 page 131
1 a   2 b   3 f   4 d   5 e   6 c

Exercise 3 page 133
1 Dubai   2 1,614   3 1,776   4 101   5 31
6 3,900,000,000

Exercise 4 page 133
1 What Are Skyscrapers?, What Are Some Famous Skyscrapers?, How Much Money Do Skyscrapers Cost?, What Is Inside a Skyscraper?
2 Para 1: very tall buildings, usually more than 984 feet,
Para 2: the Empire State Building, Shanghai World Financial Center, One World Trade Center, Burj Khalifa,
Para 3: expensive, cost more than other buildings
Para 4: floors, elevators, shopping centers

Exercise 5 page 133
1 One World Trade Center. *Answers will vary.*
2 *Answers will vary.*

3 *Answers will vary, but may include*: how the building will be used, how many people will use it, what it will be made of, where it will be located, etc.

LANGUAGE DEVELOPMENT

Exercise 1 page 134
1 The Burj Khalifa   2 One World Trade Center
3 Skyscrapers   4 The Shanghai World Financial Center

Exercise 2 page 134
1 shopping mall
2 apartments
3 garden, roof
4 stairs
5 entrance, exit
6 windows
7 ceiling
8 parking lot
9 walls
10 elevators

Exercise 3 page 135
1 parking lot
2 elevator
3 entrance
4 stairs
5 exit
6 apartment
7 walls
8 windows

Exercise 4 page 135
1 d
2 c
3 e
4 f
5 b
6 a

Exercise 5 page 135
1 expensive
2 beautiful
3 modern
4 traditional
5 cheap
6 ugly

CRITICAL THINKING

Exercise 1 page 136
1 F
2 D
3 E

Exercise 2 page 137
Answers will vary.

Exercise 3 page 137
Answers will vary.

GRAMMAR FOR WRITING

Exercise 1 page 138
1 The Burj Khalifa has more floors than One World Trade Center.
2 The Burj Khalifa has more visitors than the Shanghai World Financial Center.
3 The John Hancock Center has more stairs than the Mall of America.
4 The Burj Khalifa has more elevators than the Shanghai World Financial Center.
5 One World Trade Center cost more money than the Burj Khalifa.
6 Burj Khalifa cost less money than One World Trade Center.

Exercise 2 page 139
1 The Metropolitan Museum of Art is **more** popular **than** the Art Institute of Chicago.
2 One World Trade Center is more modern **than** the Empire State Building.
3 The John Hancock Center in Chicago is **smaller than** the Shanghai World Financial Center.
4 Modern buildings are **more beautiful than** traditional buildings.
5 The Burj Khalifa **is** taller **than** One World Trade Center.
6 Wood is more expensive **than** plastic.
7 This street is **busier** than the main road.
8 Many buildings in New York are **older** than buildings in Kansas City.

ACADEMIC WRITING SKILLS

Exercise 1 page 140
1 The Shanghai World Financial Center has over 101 floors, but One World Financial Center has more.
2 The Sears Tower is tall, but the CN Tower in Toronto is taller.
3 One World Trade Center has many elevators, but the Burj Khalifa has more.
4 The Art Institute of Chicago has many pictures, but the Metropolitan Museum of Art has more.

Exercise 2 page 141
1
✓ They are usually more than 984 feet (300 meters) tall.
✓ Many countries build skyscrapers so tourists go there.
✓ There are many skyscrapers in Asia, the Gulf, the Americas, and Europe.
2
✓ The Burj Khalifa has more elevators than One World Trade Center or the Shanghai World Financial Center.
✓ It has 57 elevators.
✓ One World Trade Center has 54 elevators but the Shanghai World Financial Center has fewer.

Exercises 3–4 page 142
Answers will vary.

WRITING TASK

Exercises 1–5 pages 142–143
Answers will vary.

ON CAMPUS

Exercise 1 page 144
Answers will vary.

Exercise 3 page 145
1 T
2 F; a professor does.
3 T
4 T
5 F; a TA does.
6 T

Exercise 4 page 145
1 lecture
2 quiz section
3 lab class
4 seminar

Exercises 5–8 page 145
Answers will vary.

UNIT 7
ACIVATE YOUR KNOWLEDGE

Exercise 1 page 147
1 selling fruit and vegetables at a market
2 tomatoes, beans, limes
3 *Answers will vary.*

WATCH AND LISTEN

Exercise 1 page 148
Answers will vary.

Exercise 2 page 148
1 village   2 fruit   3 farm   4 cheese

Exercise 3 page 149
1 3 4 6

Exercise 4 page 149
1 fruit, vegetables, bread, meat, and cheese
2 goat cheese
3 at the door
4 2 quarts
5 in another room
6 1–3 weeks

Exercise 5 page 149
1 c
2 d
3 a
4 b

Exercise 6 page 149
Answers will vary.

READING 1

Exercise 1 page 150
Answers will vary.

Exercise 2 page 150
1 e   2 c   3 g   4 a
5 b   6 d   7 f

Exercise 3 page 150
5a
3b
2c
4d
1e

Exercise 4 page 152

Country	How is the tea prepared? What do people eat with it?
Malaysia	• Pour hot water on black tea. • After five minutes, add sugar and milk. • Then 'pull' the tea (pour the tea from one cup to another many times) • eat canai bread with it.
Russia	• Use a special kettle called a samovar. • Like drinking tea with lemon • Sometimes, drink with some sugar or jam
Turkey	• Use two kettles: one for the water and one for the tea. • Drink with some sugar
Arab countries	• Made with cardamon, ginger, milk, and sugar
United Kingdom	• Add some milk and sugar • Usually eat cookies with their tea

Exercise 5 page 152
1 Malaysia (Kuala Lumpur is the capital city.)
2 Russia
3 Japan
4 Russia
5 Turkey
6 Malaysia

Exercise 6 page 152
Answers will vary.

READING 2

Exercise 1 page 153
Answers will vary.

Exercise 2 page 153
1 students   2 types of food

Exercise 3 page 153
1 f
2 c
3 d
4 b
5 e
6 a
7 g

Exercise 4 page 155
1 F; American should come before Arab.
2 F; Sharwarma is a savory meat dish.
3 F; Amok trey is a Cambodian dish.
4 T
5 T
6 T
7 F; Kangaroo burgers are served on a type of bread.

Exercise 5 page 155
1 Middle Eastern countries
2 Sharwarma and kangaroo burgers
3 crocodile and kangaroo
4 Arab and Cambodian
5 Australian and Cambodian

Exercise 6 page 156
1 meat
2 *Answers will vary.*
3 *Answers will vary.*

LANGUAGE DEVELOPMENT

Exercise 1 page 156
1 a 2 a 3 a 4 a 5 a
6 b 7 b 8 a 9 a

Exercise 2 page 157
Answers will vary.

Exercise 3 page 157
Answers will vary.

Exercise 4 page 158
Correct: 2, 5, 6
Incorrect: 1, 3, 4, 7, 8

Exercise 5 page 158
1 **Honey is** sweet.
3 **Milk is** good for children.
4 **Bread is** tasty.
7 **Fish is** good for you.
8 **Water is** served in a glass.

CRITICAL THINKING

Exercise 1 page 159
1 made of meat
2 served in a pita with vegetables
3 tastes savory

Exercise 2 page 160
Answers will vary.

Exercise 3 page 160
Answers will vary.

GRAMMAR FOR WRITING

Exercise 1 page 161
1 prepare 2 uses 3 is 4 is 5 is 6 are

Exercise 2 page 162
Correct: 2, 5
Incorrect: 1, 3, 4, 6

Exercise 3 page 162
1 Korean **restaurants serve** rice with meat and vegetables.
3 Latin American **chefs use** many different kinds of vegetables in their dishes.
4 **Hamburgers are** served in bread.
6 French vegetable **soup is** delicious.

Exercise 4 page 163
1 At **some Arab restaurants/Arab restaurants**, you can find delicious meat dishes.
2 The curry is served with **some rice/rice**.
3 **Some famous dishes** in New Orleans **are** *jambalaya* and *gumbo*.
4 French chefs add **an apple** to this dish.
5 Korean chefs prepare many dishes with **some meat/meat**.
6 **Australians** like eating **crocodile meat**.
7 There are **some vegetables/vegetables** in Korean *kimchi*
8 **A popular dish** in Latin America is chicken soup.

ACADEMIC WRITING SKILLS

Exercise 1 page 164
1 There are many tasty dishes, but this is one of the best.
2 If you like tasty meat dishes, you will enjoy your meal at an Arab restaurant.

Exercise 2 page 164
Answers will vary.

WRITING TASK

Exercises 1–6 page 165
Answers will vary.

ON CAMPUS

Exercise 1 page 166
Answers will vary.

Exercise 3 page 167

1 T
2 F; No, you can't.
3 T
4 F; only the important ideas

Exercise 4 page 167

1 c
2 e
3 d
4 b
5 a

Exercises 5–6 page 167

Answers will vary.

UNIT 8
ACIVATE YOUR KNOWLEDGE

Exercise 1 page 169

1 by boat, by car, by train
2 *Answers will vary.*
3 *Answers will vary.*

WATCH AND LISTEN

Exercise 1 page 170

Answers will vary.

Exercise 2 page 170

1 underground   2 on   3 busy   4 subway station

Exercise 3 page 170

1 T   2 F; The oldest subway system is in London.   3 T
4 F; Tokyo has the busiest subway system.   5 T

Exercise 4 page 171

1 c   2 a   3 b   4 b

Exercise 5 page 171

1 traffic   2 faster   3 usually   4 helpful

Exercise 6 page 171

Answers will vary.

READING 1

Exercise 1 page 172

1 a questionnaire / a survey
2 to get information from people

Exercise 2 page 172

1 a   2 a   3 b   4 a   5 b   6 a   7 a   8 a

Exercise 3 page 174

Topics 2, 4, and 6

Exercise 4 page 174

1 32–53   4 motorcycle
2 15–45 minutes   5 Yes
3 subway

Exercise 5 page 174

1 F; There is a place for people to write their suggestions.
2 T
3 F; The purpose is to see how people in Bangkok travel
   and how they feel about transportation in Bangkok.
4 F; She sometimes takes the bus.
5 F; She thinks more tracks for subways should be added.

Exercise 6 page 175

Answers will vary.

READING 2

Exercise 1 page 175

Weather report: information about weather
News report: information about the news
Possible answers: grade report: information about your
grades / traffic report: information about traffic

Exercise 2 page 175

1 b
2 c
3 a

Exercise 3 page 176

1 prefer
2 takes / rides
3 spends
4 report
5 results
6 drives
7 take / ride

Exercise 4 page 177

bike 2%
car 23%
tuk-tuk 8%
motorcycle 14%
bus 18%
SkyTrain 21%

Exercise 5 page 178

1 transportation
2 take
3 take
4 drive
5 traffic
6 motorcycles

Exercise 6 page 178

1 over 8 million
2 a public form of transportation
3 23 %
4 more than 1 hour
5 almost 35%

Exercise 7 page 179
1 car, *Answers will vary.*
2 *Answers will vary.*
3 *Answers will vary.*

LANGUAGE DEVELOPMENT

Exercise 1 page 179
1 quantifier: Most; noun: people
2 quantifier: Some; noun: people
3 quantifier: Not many; noun: people
4 quantifier: A few; noun: people
5 quantifier: Many; noun: people

Exercise 2 page 180
1 Many / Most / A lot of
2 Not many / A few (some)
3 some (not many, a few)
4 Not many / A few (Some)
5 Not many / A few

Exercise 3 page 181
1 We take a bus to school.
2 Melissa travels to work by train.
3 Shu takes his car to the city.
4 Many people get to work by motorcycle.
5 My children get to school by bike.
6 Suni takes a taxi to the store.

Exercise 4 page 181
1 rides
2 take
3 ride
4 takes / rides
5 drive

CRITICAL THINKING

Exercise 1 page 182
paragraphs 2 and 3

Exercise 2 page 182
1 b
2 c
3 a

Exercise 3 page 182
17% take the subway or other train.
8% take the bus.
2% ride a water taxi.
1% bike to work.
7% walk to work.
3% take a taxi to work.
63% drive to work.

Exercise 4 page 182

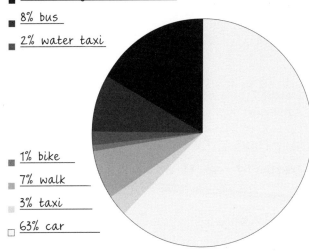

- 17% subway or other train
- 8% bus
- 2% water taxi
- 1% bike
- 7% walk
- 3% taxi
- 63% car

Exercise 5 page 183
1 by car
2 take the subway or train, take the bus, walk
3 ride a water taxi, bike, (walk), take a taxi, (take the bus)

Exercise 6 page 183
Answers will vary.

GRAMMAR FOR WRITING

Exercise 1 page 183
Sentence 2 (water taxi) and Sentence 4 (motorcycle).

Exercise 2 page 184
2 Juan drives a car to university.
4 Many people ride a bike to work in London.
5 People in Bangkok prefer to take the SkyTrain.

Exercise 3 page 184
1 In Abu Dhabi, **people drive cars** to work.
2 Not many people in Ankara take **taxis to work**.
3 Workers in Seoul take the train **to** work.
4 Most students **ride motorcycles to school**.
5 Some students in Paris take **the bus to college**.

Exercise 4 page 184
1 d
2 a
3 e
4 c
5 b

Exercise 5 page 185
1 It
2 It
3 They
4 They
5 It

ACADEMIC WRITING SKILLS

Exercise 1 page 186
1 b
2 e
3 c
4 a
5 d

Exercise 2 page 186
Answers will vary.

WRITING TASK

Exercises 1–7 pages 186–187
Answers will vary.

ON CAMPUS

Exercise 1 page 188
Answers will vary.

Exercise 3 page 189
1 c
2 a
3 c

Exercise 4 page 189
1 T
2 T
3 F; The bus not easy when she has a lot of groceries.
4 F; He can't go to the mountains by bike.
5 T
6 F; She doesn't like to take the bus at night.

Exercises 5–8 page 189
Answers will vary.

UNIT 1

▶ Thai Fishermen

Narrator: This is Goon, and this is where he lives.

He lives in a village by the sea, on an island called Ko Surin. His island is near the west coast of Thailand in Asia.

Goon and his friends are part of the Moken people. They live on land, but they spend a lot of their time in and on the sea.

The Moken people are very good at sailing, fishing, and diving. But they don't use special equipment or goggles.

They jump from their boat into the water. These boys are very good swimmers. But how can they see to find food underwater without goggles? Goon and his friends are special.

They can see everything underwater easily.

Goon can see the beautiful fish and plants around him. This helps him catch fish and other sea animals for his friends and family.

UNIT 2

▶ The Growing Ice Cap

Narrator: In the beginning of winter here, the days grow short and cold. Snow and cold temperatures move south into parts of North America, Europe, and Asia.

Winter is hard here. Water in the air, in rivers, and in plants turns to ice. As a result, most of the plants die. But some trees, like fir trees and pine trees, can live in very cold temperatures. These trees make up the greatest forest on Earth, called the taiga.

The taiga forest goes around the northern part of the Earth. From Alaska to Canada, from Scandinavia to Russia, it has almost 30% of all the trees on Earth!

During the winter, in the most northern part of the taiga forest, freezing air from the north meets warm air from the south. Heavy snow covers this area of the taiga until warmer temperatures return in the spring.

UNIT 3

▶ Panama's Kuna People

Narrator: The Kuna people live in Colombia and Panama. Almost 35,000 of them live on islands near the coast of Panama called Kuna Yala. They are people of the sea.

Many of the Kuna are fishermen. They sometimes swim more than 100 feet deep and stay underwater for two minutes at a time. They catch fish and lobsters for food.

They also get food from their islands. They grow coconuts on many of the smaller islands. Most of the people live in villages on the larger islands. They have a rich culture, and they wear colorful traditional clothes every day.

The Kuna always take care of their islands and keep their villages clean. Every morning they go to the beach and sweep the sand.

They have small gardens around their homes, and they water their plants every day. They also raise animals.

Music is important to the Kuna men, women, and children. In their free time, they often play music and dance. Their daily life is probably very different from yours and mine.

UNIT 4

▶ The Cenotes of Mexico

Narrator: In the southeast part of Mexico, known as the Yucatán, there are many rich, green forests.

Here, these amazing holes are the only spaces in the trees. They are very deep, they are made of rock, and they are often full of water. Mexicans call these places *cenotes*.

Olmo Torres-Talamante is a scientist. For him, the *cenotes* are very special. He studies them, and the plants and animals in and around them.

Water is very important in the Yucatán. It rains a lot here, but there are no lakes or rivers. When it rains, the water goes down into the rock under the Yucatán. Over time, it makes the *cenotes*.

Cenotes are the only places to find fresh water in the Yucatán. They help the animals and plants in the forest live.

Lily pads, fish, and turtles all live at the top of the *cenotes*, where it's warm and light.

But when Olmo swims deeper into the cave, it gets cold and dark. How can anything live here?

But even here, the scientist finds life.

UNIT 5

▶ Utah's Bingham Mine

Narrator: This is the Bingham copper mine in Utah, in the western United States. It's the largest mine of its kind in the world. And it gets bigger all the time. Today it's two-and-a-half miles wide and almost one mile deep.

Matt Lengerich is the operations manager of the mine. It produces enough copper each year to make wires for every home in the USA and Mexico. We use copper everywhere—in our homes, cell phones, and cars—and some of it comes from here.

But the rocks contain only a small amount of copper. So Matt's workers have to dig up a lot of rocks to get enough copper. That's why Bingham mine is so big.

Matt's workers use these giant trucks to dig up the copper. Sometimes the copper is so deep that they have to dig for seven years to reach it.

Everything about the mine is big. These giant trucks are heavier than a jumbo jet and work 24 hours a day.

Drivers use the giant trucks to move the rocks and copper.

But they also use something stronger.

The Bingham mine is more than 100 years old, and it's larger than any other mine of its kind.

UNIT 6

▶ To Build the Tallest

Narrator: For almost 4,000 years the Great Pyramid of Egypt was the world's tallest building. It is 455 feet, or almost 140 meters, tall, and it is made of stone.

Then in the year 1311, a small town in Britain finally built something taller.

The Lincoln Cathedral was also made of stone, but its makers used new ways to build it taller. With the three tall spires on top, Lincoln Cathedral was 46 feet, or 14 meters, taller than the Great Pyramid.

To build taller than the pyramids and cathedrals, we needed a new material: steel. In 1887, the Eiffel Tower in Paris, France, became almost two times taller than the Lincoln Cathedral.

In 1930, the Chrysler Building in New York City, used steel to make it the tallest skyscraper in the world.

One year later, the Empire State Building used steel to go even higher.

The next big change was in 1972 when New York's very tall World Trade Center was finished.

One year later, the Sears Tower in Chicago, Illinois, opened. Steel and glass made these buildings light.

Later, the Petronas Towers in Kuala Lumpur, Malaysia, used steel, glass, and concrete.

At 1,667 feet tall, Taipei 101 in Taipei City was the first building to be half a kilometer high. And buildings like the Burj Khalifa in Dubai, in the United Arab Emirates, keep pushing higher.

UNIT 7

▶ Goat Cheese

Narrator: This is the village of Arreau in the south of France. Every Thursday morning in Arreau, there is a market. Here, farmers sell fruit, vegetables, bread, meat, and cheese.

Cheese is very popular in France. And Arreau has some very special cheese—goat cheese.

Mrs. Tuchan sells goat cheese from her farm.

Her farm is in a village near Arreau. People can visit the farm to learn how she and her husband make cheese.

First they have to get the milk from the goats. The goats wait at the door. They go into the milking room one by one. Mrs. Tuchan uses a machine to get the milk. She does this twice a day. Each goat can give more than two quarts of milk every day.

Next, the milk goes to a different room – the cheese-making room.

Now they have to turn the milk into cheese. Mr. Tuchan adds an ingredient to the goat milk. Then, he puts it in small plastic cups with holes in the bottom.

The next day, he turns the cheese over. Then he adds some salt to it.

Next, he moves the cheese to another room. The cheese stays here for one to three weeks. Then it will be ready to sell, and to eat.

UNIT 8

 Modern Subways

Narrator: How do people in big cities travel? Many of them take the subway. Subways move millions of people underground every day. There are over 150 subway systems in the world today.

The oldest one is in London, England.

There, everyone calls it the "Tube."

At 8:00 a.m., the Tube really gets busy. In the morning, over 500,000 Londoners go to work by subway. Of course, people on the streets can't see them.

But what if the Tube ran above the ground?

Every day in London, over 500 trains on 250 miles of track move nearly 3 million people.

That's a lot of people, but the busiest subway system in the world is in Tokyo, Japan.

There are more people in Tokyo than in any other city in the world. Around 35,000 people take the Tokyo subway every hour. That means 8 million riders travel underground every day.

On every platform, there are 25 subway attendants, like Yuhei Mitsuhashi.

They keep the riders safe, calm, and on time, because the trains cannot be late.

Name: _____   Date: _____

PART A KEY SKILLS
PREVIEWING A TEXT

1 Look at the text and photo. Circle the correct words to make true sentences.

1 The photo shows a *runner / soccer player*.
2 The title of the text is *A Very Fast Man / Chapter 8*.
3 The text is from a *book / web page*.

Unusual People: Chapter 8 – The Fastest and the Slowest

A Very Fast Man!

Usain Bolt is from Jamaica. His date of birth is August 21, 1986. He lives in Kingston, Jamaica. He has one brother and one sister.

Usain is a runner. He runs very fast. He runs in the 100-meter, 200-meter, and the 4-by-100 meter relay races. He was good at running at school. Now he is the fastest runner in the world. He is called the fastest man of all time.

Usain has the fastest times for running the 100 meters and 200 meters. He has nine Olympic gold medals. Three are from the 2008 Beijing Olympics, three are from the 2012 London Olympics, and three are from the 2016 Rio de Janeiro Olympics.

Usain works very hard. He runs and he goes to the gym. He has several hobbies. He likes to play soccer. He is also interested in helping children. He gives money to hospitals. He gives money to his high school. The money helps students at the school play sports.

PART B ADDITIONAL SKILLS

2 Read the text. Then circle the correct words to complete the profile.

Profile: Usain Bolt
First name: (1) *Usain / Bolt*
Last name: (2) *Usain / Bolt*
Country: (3) *England / Jamaica*
City: (4) *London / Kingston*
Date of birth: (5) *August 21, 1968 / August 21, 1986*
Family: (6) *one brother and one sister / one brother and two sisters*
Job: (7) *runner / soccer player*
Olympic Gold medals: (8) *three / nine*
Hobbies: (9) *soccer / working at a hospital*
Interests: (10) *helping children / teaching soccer*

UNIT 1 LANGUAGE QUIZ

Name: _____ Date: _____

PART A KEY VOCABULARY

1 Write the words from the box in the blanks

city   family   hobby   interested in   job   languages   unusual

1 I have an _____ family. They are very different from other people.
2 Everyone in my family speaks five _____: English, Portuguese, French, Italian, and Romanian.
3 We are _____ other countries and cultures.
4 My sister has a _____. She likes to play soccer.
5 My brother has a _____ in Italy. He is a teacher.
6 We are from a big _____ in Portugal.
7 My _____ is very special to me.

2 Match the sentence halves.

1 My **date of birth** is _____   a TV and videos.
2 My favorite **country** is _____   b day with nice weather.
3 I like to **watch** _____   c because it sounds nice.
4 My brother **lives** _____   d Mexico because of the weather.
5 Dr. Delgado **works** _____   e in a house in Florida.
6 I like piano **music** _____   f at a hospital in San Diego.
7 It is a **normal** _____   g August 10, 2000.

PART B LANGUAGE DEVELOPMENT
FAMILY VOCABULARY

3 Write the words from the box in the blanks. You do not need every word.

aunt   brother   daughter   father   grandfather   grandmother   mother   sister   son   uncle

1 My brother is my mother's _____.   5 My mother's sister is my _____.
2 My father's father is my _____.   6 My brother's father is my _____.
3 My mother's brother is my _____.   7 My mother's mother is my _____.
4 My sister is my father's _____.   8 My father's son is my _____.

NOUNS AND VERBS

4 Write the words from the box in the blanks.

brothers   lives   sister   speak   work

1 Ali _____ in Texas with his sister.
2 My father has four _____.
3 They have one _____. Her name is Olga.
4 Her brothers _____ on a farm.
5 They _____ French and English.

UNIT 1 WRITING QUIZ

Name: _____ Date: _____

PART A GRAMMAR FOR WRITING
THE VERB *BE*

1 Write *am*, *is*, or *are* in the blanks.

1 My name _____ Tomiko.
2 I _____ 21 years old.
3 I _____ from Osaka.
4 Osaka _____ in Japan.
5 My hobbies _____ swimming and playing soccer.

SUBJECT PRONOUNS AND POSSESSIVE ADJECTIVES

2 Circle the correct words.

1 I have two brothers. *Their / They* names are Hector and Luis.
2 Flora is from Mexico. *She / Her* speaks Spanish.
3 We go to school in Michigan. *Our / His* school is very big.
4 I have a brother and a sister. *We / Our* live in Toronto.
5 Lee is from Birmingham. *Her / She* mother is from China.

PART B WRITING TASK

> Write a profile of a friend.

3 Write at least five sentences about your friend. Think about your friend's:

- name
- date of birth
- city
- country
- language
- job
- family
- hobby

_____
_____
_____
_____
_____
_____
_____
_____

Name: _____   Date: _____

PART A KEY SKILLS
SCANNING TO FIND INFORMATION

1 Scan the text. Match the facts to the correct numbers or words.

1 the warmest months _____
2 the coldest months _____
3 the average number of rainy days in January _____
4 the average rainfall in January _____
5 the average number of rainy days in July _____

a 14
b 6 inches
c 15
d January, February, March
e June, July, August

A Very Wet Town

Cilaos is one of the wettest cities in the world. It is on the French island of Réunion in the Indian Ocean.

Average Temperatures
The temperatures in Cilaos are from 60 °F (16 °C) to 77 °F (25 °C). It is warmest from January to March. The temperatures are from 72 °F (22 °C) to 77 °F (25 °C). The coldest months are from June to August. The temperatures are still nice, from 60 °F (16 °C) to 66 °F (19 °C).

Seasons
November is the beginning of the rainy season. The wettest months are January and February. There are about 15 rainy days in January. The average rainfall in January is six inches (153 mm).

"June is the start of winter here," says George, "and this is my favorite time of year." George is a farmer in Cilaos. He grows fruit. "During the dry winter months, I get the house ready for the rainy season," George says.

People in Cilaos enjoy the weather in the dry season. However, in this wet place, the dry season also has some rain. There are about 14 rainy days in July. The average rainfall in July is about two inches (57 mm).

PART B ADDITIONAL SKILLS

2 Complete the sentences with the correct months from the reading.

The average rainfall of two inches is in [1] _____.
The start of winter is [2] _____.
The beginning of the rainy season is [3] _____.
The wettest months are [4] _____ and [5] _____.

UNIT 2 LANGUAGE QUIZ

Name: _____ Date: _____

PART A KEY VOCABULARY

1 Choose the correct words to complete the sentences.

1 When it is _____, I go to the beach.
   a warm   b cold

2 I like all the _____. I enjoy the change in weather.
   a winters   b seasons

3 It is below 0°F! It is so _____!
   a dry   b cold

4 On a _____ day, I can't see the sun.
   a windy   b cloudy

5 On a _____ day, I go outside and enjoy the weather.
   a sunny   b windy

6 Some children do not go to school in the _____. Their school ends in the spring.
   a summer   b fall

7 In the _____ in North America, it is summer in South America.
   a winter   b spring

8 I am so wet! It is a very _____ day.
   a dry   b rainy

2 Match the sentence halves.

1 The **spring** _____   a there is a lot of wind.
2 On a **windy** day, _____   b is after the summer.
3 In the **dry** season, _____ c is after the winter.
4 The **fall** _____   d there is not a lot of rain.
5 We have high **rainfall** so _____   e is warm all year.
6 The **climate** in São Paolo, Brazil _____   f it is very wet.

PART B LANGUAGE DEVELOPMENT
NOUNS AND ADJECTIVES

3 Write the bold words in the correct place in the chart.

1 The **classroom** is **warm**.
2 **November** is **cloudy**.
3 The **climate** in the rainforest is **rainy**.
4 The **rainfall** in New Orleans is **high**.
5 The **spring** is **sunny**.

Adjectives	Nouns

NOUN PHRASES

4 Make a noun phrase from the bold words in each sentence. Write the noun phrase in the blanks to make a new sentence.

1 The **climate** in Spain is **good**.
   Spain has a _____.

2 In the spring, the **rainfall** is **high**.
   In the spring, there is _____.

3 **Summers** are **hot** in Chicago.
   Chicago has _____.

4 The **season** is **dry** from June to October.
   The _____ is from June to October.

5 Montreal's **winters** are **cold**.
   Montreal has _____.

UNIT 2 WRITING QUIZ

Name: _____   Date: _____

PART A GRAMMAR FOR WRITING
PREPOSITIONAL PHRASES

1 Correct the mistakes with prepositions. Use *about, between, for,* or *in.*

1 For the winter, the weather is cold.

_____

2 The average rainfall in January is between 6 inches.

_____

3 Spring lasts in three months.

_____

4 Summer in Canada is for June and August.

_____

5 The average temperatures is in 70 °F.

_____

PART B WRITING TASK

What is your favorite season?

2 Write at least five sentences about the weather in your favorite season.

- Say which months the season is in.
- Write about the weather in the season.
- Write about the average temperatures in this season.

_____
_____
_____
_____
_____
_____
_____

Name: _____   Date: _____

PART A KEY SKILLS
ANNOTATING A TEXT

1 Read the questions. Then underline the key words in the text that answer each question.

   1 What is Williams's job? (Paragraph 1)
   2 What is Paragraph 2 about?
   3 How many people work at the website with William? (Paragraph 3)
   4 How does William feel about his new job? (Paragraph 4)

William's blog

My first week at my new job

1 I started work this week as a journalist. It's my first job. It's for a news website called *The Neighborhood News*. It's in Philadelphia, Pennsylvania.

2 My schedule is busy. I get up early, and I start work at 9 a.m. I have breakfast at the office. Then I travel around the city. I usually speak to people all day. Sometimes I don't have time for lunch. I write my stories in the office. I work until late in the evening.

3 Four other people work here. Tina is the editor, and Jo and Sam are also journalists. George is the website manager. Everyone is very friendly.

4 The money isn't very good, but I'm new. I'm learning a lot and I'm becoming a better writer. I don't have time to relax, but I love my new job. I meet lots of interesting people.

2 Use the key words you underlined in Exercise 1 to summarize the text.

William is a (1) _____ with a busy (2) _____. He works with (3) _____ other people. He (4) _____ his job.

PART B ADDITIONAL SKILLS

3 Circle the correct words to make true sentences.

   1 William started a new job *this / last* week.
   2 William starts work at *8 a.m. / 9 a.m.*
   3 William has breakfast at *home / work*.
   4 William thinks everyone is *busy / friendly*.
   5 William *does / does not* have time to relax.

UNIT 3 LANGUAGE QUIZ

Name: _____ Date: _____

PART A KEY VOCABULARY

1 Complete the paragraph with the correct words in the box.

cook   evening   get up   morning   relax   schedule   swim   weekdays

I [1] _____ very early in the [2] _____. I begin work at 7 a.m. I don't have time to [3] _____ at home until about 8 p.m. in the [4] _____. Then I [5] _____ my dinner. I go to sleep and begin my [6] _____ again the next day. This is my life on the [7] _____. My life is different on Saturday and Sunday. I have time to [8] _____ at the pool and do other hobbies.

2 Circle the correct word.

1 I eat *lunch / dinner* in the middle of the day at 12 p.m.
2 On the *weekend / morning*, I don't have classes.
3 I study at the library from 2 to 4 p.m. in the *afternoon / weekday*.
4 I *meet / relax* my friends at the café. Then we walk to class.
5 My friends have *dinner / lunch* together in the evening after work.
6 On a *busy / relax* day, I go to school and then work.
7 I like to *travel / relax* to different places.

PART B LANGUAGE DEVELOPMENT
COLLOCATIONS FOR FREE-TIME ACTIVITIES

3 Match the sentence halves.

1 I get _____
2 She likes to take _____
3 He goes to _____
4 She studies _____
5 He does _____

a the bus to school.
b biology at Boston College.
c homework in the evening.
d up at 9:30 a.m.
e the gym in the morning.

4 Circle the correct words to complete the sentences.

1 I study *every / in* the afternoon.
2 My father cooks dinner *at / on* 5 p.m.
3 My brother has swim lessons *in / on* Tuesdays.
4 *On / In* Sunday night, we relax.
5 I go to the library *every / at* Thursday.

UNIT 3 WRITING QUIZ

Name: _____ Date: _____

PART A GRAMMAR FOR WRITING
PARTS OF A SENTENCE

1 Label the parts of the sentence. Write S (subject), V (verb), O (object), or PP (prepositional phrase) in the blanks.

1 _____ + _____ + _____
   Olivia   studies   economics.

2 _____ + _____ + _____
   Diego   works   in Edmonton.

3 _____ + _____ + _____ + _____
   Olga   writes   stories   for the website.

4 _____ + _____ + _____
   In the evening,   I   study.

5 _____ + _____ + _____ + _____
   In the afternoon,   I   go   to the library.

THE SIMPLE PRESENT

2 Complete the sentences with the correct forms of the verbs in parentheses.

1 I _____ to class on Monday, Wednesday, and Friday. (go)
2 Maria _____ with friends every weekend. (relax)
3 They _____ in the pool on Saturdays. (swim).
4 Marco _____ in the library on Thursday. (study)
5 We _____ dinner together in the evening. (cook)

PART B WRITING TASK

> What is your schedule?

3 Write 5 sentences about your life.

- Write a sentence about the time you get up.
- Write three sentences about what you do on the weekdays.
- Write one sentence about what you do on the weekend or in your free time.

_____
_____
_____
_____
_____
_____
_____

UNIT 4 READING QUIZ

Name: _____   Date: _____

Read the article. Then answer the questions that follow.

Piri Reis and His World Map

1   Piri Reis came from Turkey. He was born in about 1465 and died in 1555. Piri Reis traveled around the Mediterranean Sea and the Arabian Gulf. He was a famous sea captain. Today he is famous for his world map.

2   Piri Reis's world map comes from his *Book of Navigation* (1521). Most of the book is in Turkish. In the book, there is information to help travelers. There are maps of the Mediterranean Sea, the Black Sea, the Adriatic Sea, and the Caspian Sea. The maps show islands, mountains, and cities.

3   The world map shows parts of Europe, North Africa, and South America. Piri Reis used more than 20 older maps to help him draw his world map. The map also shows the Azores and the Canary Islands in the Atlantic Ocean.

4   In 1929, part of Piri Reis's world map was found in the Topkapi Palace in Istanbul. The map is the oldest Turkish world map. It is also one of the oldest maps of America.

PART A KEY SKILLS
READING FOR MAIN IDEAS

1   Write the number of the paragraph that matches each main idea.

1   Piri Reis's map of the world is the oldest Turkish world map and the oldest map of America. _____
2   In the *Book of Navigation*, there are maps of seas and other information for travelers. _____
3   Piri Reis was a Turkish sea captain who became famous for his maps. _____
4   The world map shows parts of Europe, North Africa, and South America. _____

PART B ADDITIONAL SKILLS

2   Write *T* (true) of *F* (false) next to the sentences.

_____   1   Piri Reis was born in 1555.
_____   2   Most of the *Book of Navigation* is in Turkish.
_____   3   *The Book of Navigation* shows roads.
_____   4   Piri Reis used more than 50 older maps to help him draw his world map.
_____   5   The world map shows the Azores in the Pacific Ocean.
_____   6   Today Piri Reis is famous for his maps of the different seas.

UNIT 4 LANGUAGE QUIZ

Name: _____   Date: _____

PART A KEY VOCABULARY

1 Choose the best word from the box to complete each sentence.

| lake   map   modern   mountains   oceans   popular   river   tourists |

1 The longest _____ in South America is the Amazon in Brazil.
2 I live in a _____ city. There are many new buildings and businesses.
3 The two largest _____ in the world are the Pacific and the Atlantic.
4 I don't like high places, so I don't climb _____ or go to the top of tall buildings.
5 In the summer, we swim in a small _____ by my house.
6 My father owns a _____ restaurant. On the weekends, it is full of people.
7 There are a lot of _____ in Paris. People from all over the world love to visit it.
8 Look at this old _____ of the city. Many of the roads are the same.

2 Match the sentence halves.

1 The **capital** of the United States _____   a is by boat.
2 The **sea** by my house _____   b is home to birds and animals that live in trees.
3 The **forest** _____   c is blue and beautiful.
4 The Azores Islands are **famous** _____   d city with tourists from many different countries.
5 The **beach** near my home _____   e is Washington, D.C.
6 The only way to get to the **island** _____   f is sandy and white.
7 Buenos Aires is an **international** _____   g because of their beautiful weather and beaches.

PART B LANGUAGE DEVELOPMENT
SUPERLATIVE ADJECTIVES

3 Correct the errors in superlative adjectives. Rewrite each sentence.

1 New York City is the bigger city in the United States.

   _____

2 The popularest time to visit is in the summer.

   _____

3 The famousest place to go is Central Park.

   _____

4 The city has the good food and restaurants.

   _____

5 I think the people are the more friendly in the country.

   _____

VOCABULARY FOR PLACES

4 Circle the correct words to complete the sentences.

1 It's not safe to walk on the *cliff / field*. You could fall.
2 There is a river in the *valley / sea*.
3 There are many vegetable *farms / mountains* in the country.
4 There are not many trees in the *desert / forest*.
5 It is not easy to walk up the *hills / fields* in San Francisco, California.

Prism Intro Reading and Writing © Cambridge University Press 2017 **Photocopiable**

Name: _____   Date: _____

PART A GRAMMAR FOR WRITING
THERE IS / THERE ARE

1 Put the words in the correct order to make sentences.

1 is / city / There / in / a / my / big / lake / .

_____

2 different kinds / There / over 700 / of British cheese / are / .

_____

3 Paris / many / There / in / museums / are / .

_____

4 popular / is / the Mediterranean Sea / in / There / island / a / .

_____

5 Papua New Guinea / There / in / are / over 800 languages / .

_____

ARTICLES

2 Find the mistakes. Rewrite the sentences correctly.

1 The Lake Como is in Italy.

_____

2 He comes from the Morocco.

_____

3 Lots of people live in a New York City.

_____

4 There are many modern buildings in United Arab Emirates.

_____

5 They found a ancient map.

_____

PART B WRITING TASK

> What country do you want to visit?

3 Write a paragraph about the country you want to visit. Write a topic sentence and at least three supporting sentences.

_____
_____
_____
_____
_____
_____

Name: _____ Date: _____

Read the article. Then answer the questions that follow.

Unusual Jobs

Is your job boring? Do you want a more interesting one? If so, here are some different jobs that you might like.

Zookeeper

A zookeeper must like animals. The work is hard and you have to get up early. The schedule is busy. Zookeepers must feed and clean the animals every morning and afternoon. You also have to work weekends.

Astronaut

An astronaut must be healthy and in shape. Astronauts have to know many things. They have to have a college education in science. They have to have experience as a pilot. People need to study and work for many years to be an astronaut.

Window cleaner

Window cleaners must be in shape. They have to be strong. Cleaning tall buildings is dangerous. Window cleaners must complete a class on safety. They must be okay with working in high places.

Line sitter

Do you have some time in your schedule? Are you looking for more pay? Many people don't like to stand in long lines. Your job is to stand in line for them. This job is very busy on days with big computer and technology sales. You must be okay waiting in line for hours if needed.

PART A KEY SKILLS
READING FOR DETAILS

1 Write *T* (true) or *F* (false) next to the sentences.

_____ 1 Zookeepers have to work in the morning and evening.
_____ 2 An astronaut must take a class on safety.
_____ 3 Window cleaners must be okay with being up high.
_____ 4 Astronauts must be in shape and strong.
_____ 5 Line sitters have to work every weekend when you stand in line.

PART B ADDITIONAL SKILLS

2 Write the name of the job that matches each statement. You will use one job more than once.

zookeeper   astronaut   window cleaner   line sitter

1 This job is dangerous. _____
2 You need a college education. _____
3 You are very busy on days with big sales. _____
4 You have to get up early. _____
5 Your schedule is busy. _____

Name: _____ Date: _____

PART A KEY VOCABULARY

1 Choose the best word to complete each sentence.

1 I am a *healthy / interesting* person. I eat well, get sleep, and exercise.
2 My sister is very *friendly / good at*. She talks to everyone she meets.
3 My brother is a *teacher / nurse*. He works with doctors at a health center.
4 My mother has a *company / hospital* that sells pianos and other musical instruments.
5 My brother is a student in *high school / center*.
6 My friend is a *great / healthy* person. He is smart and helpful.
7 I work at a language *center / hospital*. We teach Japanese, Korean, and Chinese.
8 I speak four languages. I'm *good at / great* language learning.

2 Match the questions to the answers.

1 Do you work in a **hospital**? _____
2 Are you **in shape**? _____
3 Are you a **teacher**? _____
4 Do you have to take **medicine**? _____
5 Is your job **interesting**? _____
6 Is your **pay** good? _____
7 Are you studying to be an **engineer**? _____
8 Are you a **pilot**? _____

a Yes, I run every day.
b No, I don't make a lot of money.
c No, I'm not a doctor or a nurse. I work in a school.
d Yes, I want to design and build cars.
e Yes, I teach at the university.
f Yes, I fly planes for a big company.
g Yes, I talk to many people and I learn a lot.
h No, I'm not sick.

PART B LANGUAGE DEVELOPMENT
VOCABULARY FOR JOBS

3 Match the jobs to the definitions.

1 A manager _____
2 A farmer _____
3 A doctor _____
4 A journalist _____
5 A software engineer _____

a works with computers and computer programs.
b writes news stories.
c grows food and takes care of animals.
d takes care of people and gives them medicine.
e works with people in an office.

4 Circle the best words or phrases to complete the sentences.

1 A nurse has to be good with *food / people*.
2 A dancer has to be healthy and *helpful / strong*.
3 A teacher has to be *good with / good at* children.
4 A writer must be *good with / good at* writing.
5 A basketball player must be *in shape / friendly*.

Name: _____ Date: _____

PART A GRAMMAR FOR WRITING
THE PRONOUN YOU

1 Rewrite the sentences with *you* as the subject of each sentence.

1 Teachers must be friendly and have experience.

_____

2 She must speak Spanish and English.

_____

3 Pilots have to work weekends and nights.

_____

4 A nurse has to work in the evening.

_____

5 He does not have to work Monday or Wednesday.

_____

MUST AND HAVE TO

2 Put the words in the correct order to make sentences.

1 be / good / have / people / with / to / Nurses / .

_____

2 do / Teachers / have to / work / not / weekends / on / .

_____

3 An / must / good / engineer / math / at / be / .

_____

4 must / You / have / another job / not / .

_____

5 has / job / The / interesting / be / to / .

_____

PART B WRITING TASK

Write an email about a job you want.

3 Write 6–8 sentences. Describe the job to your friend. Think about the answers to these questions.

- What is the job?
- Where is the job?
- What do you need to be good at?
- What is the pay?
- When do you work?

_____
_____
_____
_____
_____
_____
_____

Name: _____ Date: _____

PART A KEY SKILLS
PREDICTING CONTENT USING VISUALS

1 Look at the photos to predict what the text is about. Check the statements you agree with.

1 The text is about a modern city. ☐
2 This is not a place for tourists. ☐
3 The text is about buildings. ☐
4 The text is about an interesting place. ☐
5 The text is about different jobs. ☐

Read the article and check your answers in Exercise 1.

Aït Benhaddou

What is Aït Benhaddou?

Aït Benhaddou is a village in Morocco. It is in the High Atlas Mountains next to the Ounila River. There is a high wall around the village and there are tall towers at the corners of the wall. Inside the wall, there are many buildings close together. The wall and the buildings are made from earth. People often have to be rebuild the buildings because of the rain.

Who built Aït Benhaddou?

The Berber people of North Africa built Aït Benhaddou. They built many towns and villages in the Atlas Mountains. There are more than 1,000 villages in the area. Some families still live in the old village of Aït Benhaddou. Most people now live in a newer village on the other side of the river.

Why is Aït Benhaddou famous?

Aït Benhaddou is famous for its southern Moroccan architecture. Most of the buildings inside the wall are houses. Some are traditional but some look like small castles. All of the homes are made from earth and wood. In the past, Aït Benhaddou was a place for travelers to stay on their way from the Sahara Desert to Marrakesh in Morocco. Now many tourists come to visit Aït Benhaddou. They want to see this village from the past.

PART B ADDITIONAL SKILLS

2 Scan the text for the words in the box. Then complete the sentences with the correct words.

High Atlas Mountains   Marrakesh   Morocco   North Africa   Ounila River

1 Aït Benhaddou is a village in the country of _____.
2 The Berber people are from _____.
3 Travelers from the Sahara Desert to _____ stayed in the village.
4 The village is next to the _____ in the _____.

Name: _____   Date: _____

PART A KEY VOCABULARY

1 Choose the best words to complete the sentences.

1 Don't break that table! It's made of _____.
  a wood   b glass

2 I live in an _____ in the city.
  a elevator   b apartment

3 We have a beautiful _____ with many flowers.
  a garden   b roof

4 You can use the _____ to get to the top of the tower.
  a wall   b elevator

5 It _____ a lot of money to build a new house.
  a expensive   b costs

6 I can hear the rain falling on the _____.
  a roof   b wall

7 We use _____ plates when we eat outside so we can throw them away.
  a glass   b plastic

8 I want a house with more _____ so we get more sunlight.
  a walls   b windows

2 Match the question to the answer.

1 Is your father **tall**? _____   a Yes, I put it up yesterday.
2 Is that a new picture on the **wall**? _____   b No, it didn't cost a lot.
3 Was your new car **expensive**? _____   c No, it cost more than $100!
4 Do you like that **building**? _____   d Yes, he is over 6 feet.
5 Is this floor real **wood**? _____   e Yes, I do. It has a beautiful design.
6 Was the restaurant meal **cheap**? _____   f Yes, it is. It's made from pine trees.

PART B LANGUAGE DEVELOPMENT
PRONOUNS

3 Circle the correct words to complete the sentences.

1 I don't have much money so I found a (1) *cheap / expensive* apartment. (2) *It / They* is great.

2 That building is made from glass and looks very (3) *modern / traditional*. (4) *It / They* was built this year.

3 I don't like looking out the window at the parking lots. (5) *They / It* are so (6) *ugly / beautiful*.

4 I visited a (7) *traditional / modern* village from the 1500s. (8) *It / They* was really interesting.

5 I can't live in the city because apartments are too (9) *cheap / expensive*. (10) *It / They* cost over $3,000 a month.

VOCABULARY FOR BUILDINGS

4 Choose the correct word from the box to complete the paragraph.

stairs   entrance   exit   parking lot   ceiling

When you get to the hotel, you can leave your car in the underground (1) _____. After you park, walk up the (2) _____ to the first floor. Then go in through the main (3) _____. Look up and you will see a beautiful glass (4) _____. It lets the sun in. On your right, there's a small café. You can enjoy a coffee there in the morning. There is a(n) (5) _____ from the building next to the café. It leads to the swimming pool.

Name: _____ Date: _____

PART A GRAMMAR FOR WRITING
COMPARING QUANTITIES; COMPARATIVE ADJECTIVES

1 Correct the mistakes in the sentences.

1 The Metropolitan Museum of Art is more popular the Museum of Modern Art.
_____

2 The Shard in London is more small the Burj Khalifa.
_____

3 Skyscrapers are uglyer that traditional buildings.
_____

4 Los Angeles is big than Chicago.
_____

5 An apartment downtown is expensiver than an apartment outside of the city.
_____

6 London has less rainy days than Portland.
_____

7 Miami is sunny more than Seattle.
_____

8 My apartment cost fewer money that your apartment.
_____

9 The museum has less elevators than the train station.
_____

10 The book gives fewer information about architecture than art history.
_____
_____

PART B WRITING TASK

Compare two buildings in your city or country.

2 Write a paragraph about two buildings. You can compare museums, restaurants, schools, or other buildings. Include the following information:

- Write the names of your buildings.
- Write what city they are in.
- Compare the height of your buildings.
- Compare the number of floors in your buildings.
- Compare the number of elevators in your buildings.
- Compare other information you have.

Name: _____ Date: _____

Read the article and answer the questions that follow.

Coffee

1 Every day all over the world, people drink more than two billion cups of coffee! Coffee has a special smell and flavor. But what is coffee, and where does it come from? How long has it been popular?

2 Coffee is made from a seed. The coffee seed is inside a fruit that grows on the coffee tree. The seed is called a *coffee bean*. Farmers grow coffee trees in the Caribbean, South America, Central America, Southeast Asia, India, and Africa. Coffee is an important business for countries in these areas.

3 Some people say that the history of coffee began in Africa. They say that people in Ethiopia were the first to drink coffee. Others say that coffee farming began in southern Arabia. We do know that in the 1400s, people enjoyed coffee in Yemen. From there, coffee became popular in the Arab world and in Europe. People went to coffee houses to drink coffee and talk with others. In the 1700s, explorers brought the coffee tree to the Americas. Soon after, it became a popular drink there.

4 Coffee is served in different ways and at different times. Some people add milk and sugar to it. You can drink it hot or cold. Many people drink coffee in the morning. Others enjoy a cup at work in the middle of the day. People also have coffee after a meal, especially at restaurants.

PART A KEY SKILLS
TAKING NOTES

1 Complete the notes with the names of places from the text.

History of coffee

- 1st place people drank coffee was probably in: (1) _____
- coffee farming began in: Africa or (2) _____
- 1400s, people enjoyed coffee in: (3) _____
- coffee became popular in: Arab world and (4) _____
- 1700s, explorers brought coffee to: (5) _____

PART B ADDITIONAL SKILLS

2 Write *T* (true) or *F* (false) next to the statements.

_____ 1 The coffee seed grows in the ground.
_____ 2 People drink more than two billion cups of coffee every day.
_____ 3 Coffee farms are popular in Europe.
_____ 4 People drank coffee in Europe before America.
_____ 5 People drink coffee at different times of the day.

Name: _____   Date: _____

PART A KEY VOCABULARY

1 Choose the best words to complete the paragraph.

> This restaurant does not [1] *serve / give* breakfast. You can only get [2] *meals / drinks* there for lunch or dinner. I don't eat [3] *meat / fish* because I don't like chicken, beef, or ham. However, this restaurant has a number of vegetarian [4] *dishes / bread* without it. For example, you can order many [5] *different / same* noodle dishes. They come with lots of [6] *vegetables / drinks*. My favorite are the cooked carrots. They also bake [7] *bread / honey* in the restaurant kitchen. It is fresh and delicious, and it smells so good. I really enjoy the food here!

2 Match the sentence halves.

1 We eat a lot of **rice** _____
2 My family eats a lot of **fish** _____
3 My favorite **drink** is _____
4 I **prepare** dinner _____
5 I eat the **same** food _____
6 I like **honey** _____
7 I eat every **type** _____

a because we live by the ocean.
b in my tea because it's sweet.
c in Japan because it grows here.
d for my family at home after work.
e tea with milk.
f every morning for breakfast.
g of fruit, but bananas are my favorite.

PART B LANGUAGE DEVELOPMENT
VOCABULARY ABOUT FOOD

3 Choose the correct word from the box to complete the paragraph.

good	made with	savory	served with	sweet

> We own a new coffee shop. Our coffee is [1] _____ beans from Columbia. Come and enjoy a cup. It is [2] _____ milk and sugar. Enjoy it with something [3] _____. We have cakes, cookies, and other desserts. You can also get something that is [4] _____ for you. We have fresh fruit, yogurt, and orange juice. If you want something more [5] _____, we have homemade bread. It is not too sweet. Everything is delicious!

COUNT AND NONCOUNT NOUNS

4 Write the nouns in the box in the correct place in the chart.

bread	honey	meal	milk	vegetable

count	non-count

Name: _____ Date: _____

PART A GRAMMAR FOR WRITING
SUBJECT-VERB AGREEMENT

1 Circle the correct verb form.

1 Arab restaurants *serves / serve* shawarma and kabsa.
2 Cambodian dishes *uses / use* a lot of fruit.
3 Fish *is / are* popular in many restaurants in Greece.

4 Thai food *is / are* served with rice and vegetables.
5 Vegetables *is/ are* very good served with rice.

DETERMINERS: *A, AN,* AND *SOME*

2 Correct the underlined parts of the sentences.

1 <u>Some popular rice dish</u> in Spain is *paella*.
_____

2 We like <u>a vegetables</u> with meat.
_____

3 Chefs prepare <u>some popular dish</u> with spices.
_____

4 The chicken is served <u>with a bread</u>.
_____

5 Can I get <u>a honey</u> for my tea?
_____

PART B WRITING TASK

What is your favorite dish at a restaurant?

3 Write a paragraph with a topic sentence, at least three supporting sentences, and a concluding sentence. Include the following information:

- the name of the dish
- the taste of the dish
- what the dish is made of
- what the dish is served in or served with

_____
_____
_____
_____
_____
_____
_____

Name: _____   Date: _____

Read the article and answer the questions that follow.

Space Tourism

1 Are you looking for a different type of trip? Do you prefer doing something exciting rather than something relaxing? Do you dream of going to the moon or to Mars? Why not try space tourism?

2 Space tourism means traveling into space. It started in 2001 with visits to the International Space Station.

3 The first space tourist was Dennis Tito, who is an American businessman. He studied engineering, and he was interested in space travel. It was his dream to go to space, and he spent eight days on the International Space Station. The trip was very expensive. It cost about $20 million. Tito was the 415th person to go to space, but he was the first non-astronaut to do it. He was 60 years old at the time.

4 The Russian space program sent eight people, including Tito, to space between 2001 and 2009. Then in 2009, Russia stopped its space tourism program so that astronauts and scientists could use the space station. Russia now has plans for more flights for tourists. As a result, more people will be able to fly through space. If you want to see a view of the Earth from a spacecraft, you may be able to soon…if you have enough money.

PART A KEY SKILLS
SKIMMING A TEXT

1 Skim the text. Write the number of the paragraph that matches the main idea.

a gives the definition of space tourism _____
b describes the Russian space tourism program _____
c gives information about the first space tourist _____
d asks the readers about their interests _____

PART B ADDITIONAL SKILLS

2 Write *T* (true) or *F* (false) next to the statements.

_____ 1 The text is about how astronauts work in space.
_____ 2 The first space tourists went to the International Space Station in 2009.
_____ 3 Dennis Tito is a Russian businessman.
_____ 4 Dennis Tito was the 8th person to go into space.
_____ 5 Only tourists visit the International Space Station now.
_____ 6 Russia plans to start its space tourism program again in the future.

Name: _____ Date: _____

PART A KEY VOCABULARY

1 Choose the best words to complete the sentences.

1 Does the _____ go to the airport or do we have to drive?
   a train   **b** bike

2 I _____ to fly. I don't like to be in the car for a long time.
   a prefer   **b** spend

3 Which way is this _____ going? I need to get downtown.
   a transportation   **b** bus

4 My son can _____, but I never let him take our car.
   a bike   **b** drive

5 Can you _____ the bus to school? It's too cold for us to walk.
   a drive   **b** take

6 I don't take _____ for short trips because they're too expensive. I ride the bus or walk instead.
   a taxis   **b** motorcycles

7 My dad got a car instead of a _____ so we can all ride together.
   a motorcycle   **b** train

8 I _____ the train so I can read a book on the way to work.
   a drive   **b** ride

2 Match the questions and answers.

1 Do you take the **subway**? _____
2 Is there a lot of **traffic** today? _____
3 Did you write your **report**? _____
4 Do you ride your **bike** to work? _____
5 Do you **spend** a lot of time driving? _____
6 Did you get your **results**? _____
7 Does your job pay for **transportation**? _____

a Yes, I enjoy the exercise.
b Yes, I get train tickets every month.
c Yes, because it's fast and clean.
d No, the roads are clear.
e Yes, I passed my driving test.
f Yes, it's about the results of a survey.
g Yes, I'm in the car for two hours every day.

PART B LANGUAGE DEVELOPMENT
QUANTIFIERS

3 Look at the percentages. Then choose the correct quantifiers to complete the sentences.

1 (83%) *Most / A few* people in Florida drive to work.
2 (4%) *A few / Many* people in Florida walk to work.
3 (2%) *Not many / Many* people in Florida take public transportation to work.
4 (74%) *Many / Some* people in California drive to work.
5 (30%) *A lot of / Some* people in Atlanta take public transportation to work.

TRANSPORTATION COLLOCATIONS

4 Correct the errors in the underlined parts of the sentences.

1 Many people travel to work <u>with subway</u>.

   _____

2 I <u>drive a taxi</u> to work.

   _____

3 On nice days, I <u>drive my motorcycle</u>.

   _____

4 People get to school <u>on bus</u>.

   _____

5 I <u>ride a car</u> on long trips.

   _____

Name: _____   Date: _____

PART A GRAMMAR FOR WRITING
SUBJECT-VERB-OBJECT

1 Put the words in the correct order to make sentences.

1 students / bus/ A few / the / take / .

_____

2 many / train / travel / by / people / In Japan, / .

_____

3 take / In Paris, / a lot of / people / subway / the / .

_____

4 people / ride / In Saigon, / to work / motorcycles / .

_____

5 In college, / bikes/ ride / most students / .

_____

LINKING SENTENCES WITH PRONOUNS

2 Look at the words in bold. Match the sentence to the sentence with the correct pronoun.

1 Jane goes to work on foot. _____
2 Sarah and Vanessa drive to college. _____
3 Hans rides his bicycle to work in Amsterdam. _____
4 Many people in New York take the bus. _____
5 People in London take the subway. _____

a They listen to music in the car.
b It is faster than the bus.
c She likes walking.
d He cycles on special roads for bikes.
e They prefer to ride than to drive.

PART B WRITING TASK

Write a paragraph about the results of a transportation survey.

3 Explain the results of the survey. Write a paragraph and include a topic sentence, at least five supporting sentences about the survey results, and a concluding sentence.

SURVEY OF SPRINGFIELD RESIDENTS

How do you get to work?	
by car	58%
by train	18%
by bus	15%
by bike	6%
on foot	3%

_____

_____

_____

_____

_____

_____

UNIT 1 READING QUIZ
PART A KEY SKILLS

1 1 runner   2 A Very Fast Man   3 book

PART B ADDITIONAL SKILLS

2 1 Usain   2 Bolt   3 Jamaica   4 Kingston
5 August 21, 1986   6 one brother and one sister
7 runner   8 nine   9 soccer   10 helping children

UNIT 1 LANGUAGE QUIZ
PART A KEY VOCABULARY

1 1 unusual   2 languages   3 interested in   4 hobby
5 job   6 city   7 family

2 1 g   2 d   3 a   4 e   5 f   6 c   7 b

PART B LANGUAGE DEVELOPMENT

3 1 son   2 grandfather   3 uncle   4 daughter
5 aunt   6 father   7 grandmother   8 brother

4 1 lives   2 brothers   3 sister   4 work   5 speak

UNIT 1 WRITING QUIZ
PART A GRAMMAR FOR WRITING

1 1 is   2 am   3 am   4 is   5 are
2 1 Their   2 She   3 Our   4 We   5 Her

PART B WRITING TASK

3 *Answers will vary.*

UNIT 2 READING QUIZ
PART A KEY SKILLS

1 1 d   2 e   3 c   4 b   5 a

PART B ADDITIONAL SKILLS

2 1 July   2 June   3 November   4 January
5 February

UNIT 2 LANGUAGE QUIZ
PART A KEY VOCABULARY

1 1 a   2 b   3 b   4 b   5 a   6 a   7 a   8 b
2 1 c   2 a   3 d   4 b   5 f   6 e

PART B LANGUAGE DEVELOPMENT

3 Adjectives: warm, cloudy, rainy, high, sunny
Nouns: classroom, November, climate, rainfall, spring

4 1 good climate   2 high rainfall   3 hot summers
4 dry season   5 cold winters

UNIT 2 WRITING QUIZ
PART A GRAMMAR FOR WRITING

1 1 **In** the winter, the weather is cold.
2 The average rainfall in January is **about** 6 inches.
3 Spring lasts **for** three months.
4 Summer in Canada is **between** June and August.
5 The average temperatures is **about** 70 °F.

PART B WRITING TASK

2 *Answers will vary.*

UNIT 3 READING QUIZ
PART A KEY SKILLS

1 1 journalist   2 schedule   3 four   4 love
2 1 journalist   2 schedule   3 four   4 loves

PART B ADDITIONAL SKILLS

3 1 this   2 9 a.m.   3 work   4 friendly   5 does not

UNIT 3 LANGUAGE QUIZ
PART A KEY VOCABULARY

1 1 get up   2 morning   3 relax   4 evening   5 cook
6 schedule   7 weekdays   8 swim

2 1 lunch   2 weekend   3 afternoon   4 meet
5 dinner   6 busy   7 travel

PART B LANGUAGE DEVELOPMENT

3 1 d   2 a   3 e   4 b   5 c
4 1 in the   2 at   3 on   4 On   5 every

UNIT 3 WRITING QUIZ
PART A GRAMMAR FOR WRITING

1 1 S+V+O
2 S+V+PP
3 S+V+O+PP
4 PP+S+V
5 PP+S+V+PP

2 1 go   2 relaxes   3 swim   4 studies   5 cook

PART B WRITING TASK

3 *Answers will vary.*

UNIT 4 READING QUIZ
PART A KEY SKILLS

1 1 4   2 2   3 1   4 3

PART B ADDITIONAL SKILLS

2 1 F; He was born in about 1465.
2 T
3 F; The maps show islands, mountains, and cities.
4 F; Piri Reis used more than 20 older maps to help him draw his world map.
5 F; The map also shows the Azores and the Canary Islands in the Atlantic Ocean.
6 F; Today he is famous for his world map.

UNIT 4 LANGUAGE QUIZ
PART A KEY VOCABULARY

1 1 river   2 modern   3 oceans   4 mountains
5 lake   6 popular   7 tourists   8 map

2 1 e   2 c   3 b   4 g   5 f   6 a   7 d

PART B LANGUAGE DEVELOPMENT

3 1 New York City is the biggest city in the U.S.
2 The most popular time to visit is in the summer.
3 The most famous place to go is Central Park.
4 The city has the best food and restaurants.
5 I think the people are the friendliest in the country.

4 1 cliff   2 valley   3 farms   4 desert   5 hills

UNIT 4 WRITING QUIZ
PART A GRAMMAR FOR WRITING

1 1 There is a big lake in my city.
2 There are over 700 different kinds of British cheese.
3 There are many museums in Paris.
4 There is a popular island in the Mediterranean Sea.
5 There are over 800 languages in Papua New Guinea.

2 1 ~~The~~ Lake Como is in Italy.
2 He comes from ~~the~~ Morocco.
3 Lots of people live in ~~a~~ New York City.
4 There are many modern buildings in **the** United Arab Emirates.
5 They found a**n** ancient map.

PART B WRITING TASK

3 *Answers will vary.*

UNIT 5 READING QUIZ
PART A KEY SKILLS

1 1 F; Zookeepers have to work every morning and afternoon.
2 F; An astronaut must have a college education in science.
3 T
4 F; An astronaut must be healthy and in shape.
5 F; This job is very busy on days with big computer and technology sales.

PART B ADDITIONAL SKILLS

2 1 window cleaner   2 astronaut   3 line sitter
4 zookeeper   5 zookeeper

UNIT 5 LANGUAGE QUIZ
PART A KEY VOCABULARY

1 1 healthy   2 friendly   3 nurse   4 company
5 high school   6 great   7 center   8 good at

2 1 c   2 a   3 e   4 h   5 g   6 b   7 d   8 f

PART B LANGUAGE DEVELOPMENT

3 1 e   2 c   3 d   4 b   5 a

4 1 people   2 strong   3 good with   4 good at
5 in shape

UNIT 5 WRITING QUIZ
PART A GRAMMAR FOR WRITING

1 1 You must be friendly and have experience.
2 You must speak Spanish and English.
3 You have to work weekends and nights.
4 You have to work in the evening.
5 You do not have to work Monday or Wednesday.

2 1 Nurses have to be good with people.
2 Teachers do not have to work on weekends.
3 An engineer must be good at math.
4 You must not have another job.
5 The job has to be interesting.

PART B WRITING TASK

3 *Answers will vary.*

UNIT 6 READING QUIZ
PART A KEY SKILLS

1 1 F; The text is about an old village.
  2 F; Now many tourists come to visit Aït Benhaddou.
  3 T
  4 T
  5 F; The text is about traditional buildings.

PART B ADDITIONAL SKILLS

2 1 Morocco   2 North Africa   3 Marrakesh
  4 Ounila River; High Atlas Mountains

UNIT 6 LANGUAGE QUIZ
PART A KEY VOCABULARY

1 1 b   2 b   3 a   4 b   5 b   6 a   7 b   8 b

2 1 d   2 a   3 b   4 e   5 f   6 c

PART B LANGUAGE DEVELOPMENT

3 1 cheap   2 It   3 modern   4 It   5 They   6 ugly
  7 traditional   8 It   9 expensive   10 They

4 1 parking lot   2 stairs   3 entrance   4 ceiling
  5 exit

UNIT 6 WRITING QUIZ
PART A GRAMMAR FOR WRITING

1 1 The Metropolitan Museum of Art is <u>more popular than</u> the Museum of Modern Art.
  2 The Shard in London is <u>smaller than</u> the Burj Khalifa.
  3 Skyscrapers are <u>uglier than</u> traditional buildings.
  4 Los Angeles is <u>bigger</u> than Chicago.
  5 An apartment downtown is <u>more expensive</u> than an apartment outside of the city.
  6 London has <u>fewer</u> rainy days than Portland.
  7 Miami is <u>sunnier</u> than Seattle.
  8 My apartment cost <u>less money than</u> your apartment.
  9 The museum has <u>fewer</u> elevators than the train station.
  10 The book gives <u>less</u> information about architecture than art history.

PART B WRITING TASK

2 *Answers will vary.*

UNIT 7 READING QUIZ
PART A KEY SKILLS

1 1 Ethiopia   2 southern Arabia   3 Yemen
  4 Europe   5 the Americas

2 1 F; The coffee seed is inside a fruit that grows on the coffee tree.
  2 T
  3 F; Farmers grow coffee trees in the Caribbean, South America, Central America, Southeast Asia, India, and Africa.
  4 T
  5 T

UNIT 7 LANGUAGE QUIZ
PART A KEY VOCABULARY

1 1 serve   2 meals   3 meat   4 dishes   5 different
  6 vegetables   7 bread

2 1 c   2 a   3 e   4 d   5 f   6 b   7 g

PART B LANGUAGE DEVELOPMENT

3 1 made with   2 served with   3 sweet   4 good
  5 savory

4 count: meal, vegetable
  non-count: bread, honey, milk

UNIT 7 WRITING QUIZ
PART A GRAMMAR FOR WRITING

1 1 serve   2 use   3 is   4 is   5 are

2 1 A popular rice dish
  2 vegetables
  3 some popular dishes / a popular dish / popular dishes
  4 with bread
  5 (some) honey

PART B WRITING TASK

3 *Answers will vary.*

UNIT 8 READING QUIZ
PART A KEY SKILLS

1 a 2 b 4 c 3 d 1

2 1 F; The text is about space tourism.
   2 F; The first space tourists went to the International
      Space in 2001.
   3 F; Dennis Tito is an American businessman.
   4 F; Tito was the 415th person to go to space.
   5 F; Astronauts and scientists visit the space station.
   6 T

UNIT 8 LANGUAGE QUIZ
PART A KEY VOCABULARY

1 1 a 2 a 3 b 4 b 5 b 6 a 7 a 8 b

2 1 c 2 d 3 f 4 a 5 g 6 e 7 b

PART B LANGUAGE DEVELOPMENT

3 1 Most   2 A few   3 Not many   4 Many   5 Some

4 1 by subway   2 take a taxi   3 ride my motorcycle
   4 by bus   5 drive (a car) / take a car

UNIT 8 WRITING QUIZ
PART A GRAMMAR FOR WRITING

1 1 A few students take the bus.
   2 In Japan, many people travel by train.
   3 In Paris, a lot of people take the subway.
   4 In Saigon, people ride motorcycles to work.
   5 In college, most students ride bikes.

2 1 c 2 a 3 d 4 e 5 b

PART B WRITING TASK

3 *Answers will vary.*

CREDITS

The authors and publishers acknowledge the following sources of copyright material and are grateful for the permissions granted. While every effort has been made, it has not always been possible to identify the sources of all the material used, or to trace all copyright holders. If any omissions are brought to our notice, we will be happy to include the appropriate acknowledgements on reprinting and in the next update to the digital edition, as applicable.

Photo credits
Key: T = Top, B = Below

p. 38: Christian Petersen/Getty Images Sport/Getty Images; p. 53 (T): Pavliha/iStock/Getty Images Plus/Getty Images; p. 53 (B): AGF/Universal Images Group Editorial/Getty Images; p. 59: Carlos Clarivan/Science Photo Library/Getty Images;

Front cover photographs by (girl) BestPhotoStudio/Shutterstock and (BG) Andrei Medvedev/Shutterstock.

Corpus
Development of this publication has made use of the Cambridge English Corpus (CEC). The CEC is a multi-billion word computer database of contemporary spoken and written English. It includes British English, American English, and other varieties of English. It also includes the Cambridge Learner Corpus, developed in collaboration with the University of Cambridge ESOL Examinations. Cambridge University Press has built up the CEC to provide evidence about language use that helps to produce better language teaching materials

Cambridge Dictionaries
Cambridge dictionaries are the world's most widely used dictionaries for learners of English. The dictionaries are available in print and online at dictionary.cambridge.org. Copyright © Cambridge University Press, reproduced with permission.

Typeset by emc design ltd